RISE

OF THE

DUNGEON

MASTER

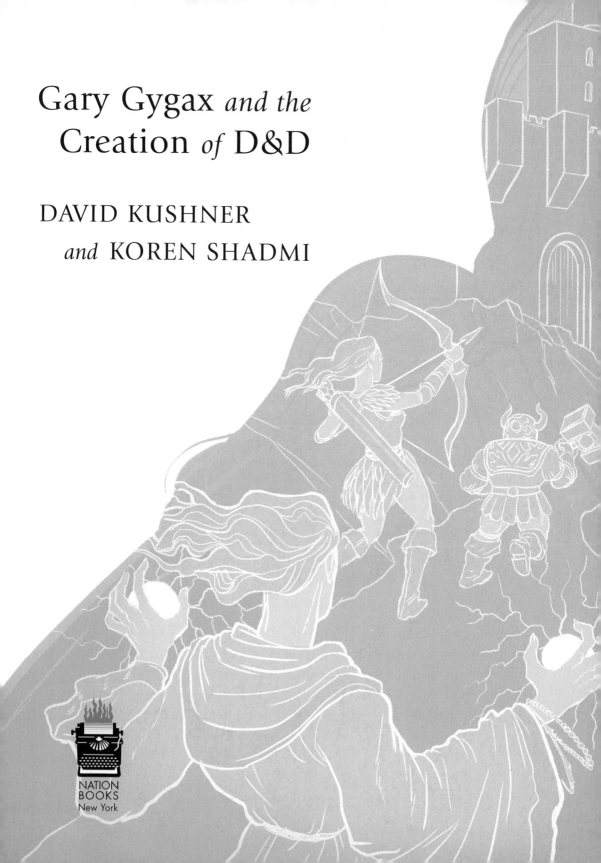

Gary Gygax *and the* Creation *of* D&D

DAVID KUSHNER
and KOREN SHADMI

NATION
BOOKS
New York

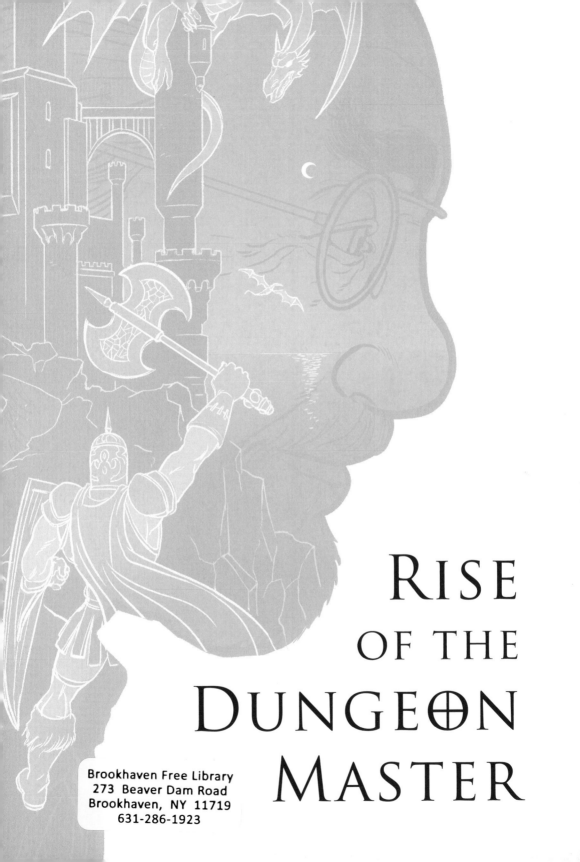

RISE
OF THE
DUNGEON
MASTER

KOREN SHADMI:

*I would like to thank Mary Abramson,
Steve Brodner, and Liad Shadmi.*

DAVID KUSHNER:

*Special thanks to Alessandra Bastagli,
Koren Shadmi, and David McCormick.*

This book is dedicated to my mom.

Published by Nation Books, A Member of the Perseus Books Group
116 East 16th Street, 8th Floor
New York, NY 10003

Nation Books is a co-publishing venture of the Nation Institute and the Perseus Books Group.

Designed by Koren Shadmi

A CIP catalog record for this book is available from the Library of Congress.

ISBN: 978-1-56858-559-8 (PB)
ISBN: 978-1-56858-560-4 (EB)

10 9 8 7 6 5 4 3 2 1

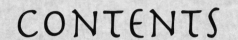

CONTENTS

CHAPTER ONE

YOU ARRIVE AT A SMALL TOWN BY A LARGE LAKE.

DOWN A ROAD, THERE IS A YELLOW VICTORIAN HOUSE WITH AN AMERICAN FLAG.

THERE ARE REVELERS HERE.

THEY STAND ON THE FRONT LAWN SWILLING ALE AND EATING FROM BOUNTIFUL PLATES OF HAM AND BEANS.

THEY INVITE YOU TO JOIN THEIR ASSEMBLY.

AS YOU APPROACH, SOMETHING CATCHES YOUR ATTENTION:

A STRANGE BUZZING SOUND IN THE AIR.

BZZZZZZZZ

BZZZZZZZZ

IT'S COMING FROM TINY WINGED BEASTS THAT ARE HANGING FROM THE TREES,

CRAWLING ALONG THE GROUND, AND CRASHING CLUMSILY AGAINST YOU.

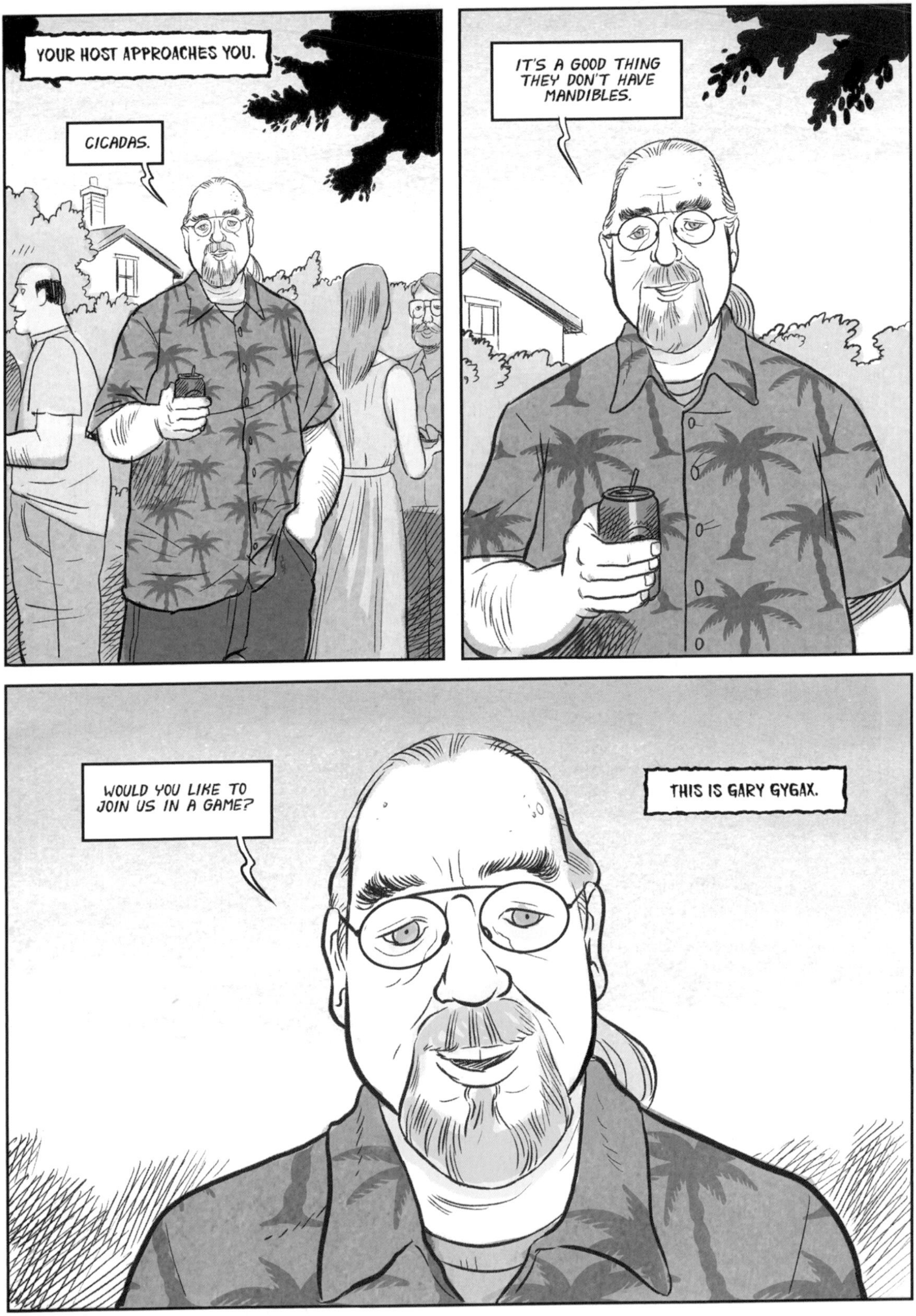
YOUR HOST APPROACHES YOU.
CICADAS.
IT'S A GOOD THING THEY DON'T HAVE MANDIBLES.
WOULD YOU LIKE TO JOIN US IN A GAME?
THIS IS GARY GYGAX.

THE OCCASION IS A GAME CONVENTION IN HIS HOMETOWN OF LAKE GENEVA, WISCONSIN, IN THE SUMMER OF 2007.

WELCOME TO LAKE GENEVA GAMING CONVENTION

GYGAX, 68, IS THE COCREATOR OF ONE OF THE MOST INFLUENTIAL GAMES EVER MADE:

DUNGEONS & DRAGONS.

BASIC SET

TSR

DUNGEONS & DRAGONS

FANTASY ADVENTURE GAME

D&D ISN'T A STRAIGHTFORWARD BOARD GAME LIKE MONOPOLY OR CLUE.

IT'S MORE LIKE AN OPERATING SYSTEM,

AN ELABORATE FRAMEWORK ON WHICH PLAYERS CAN BUILD THEIR OWN SCENARIOS.

ANYONE WITH CREATIVITY AND IMAGINATION CAN BECOME A GAME DESIGNER.

D&D PLAYERS CREATE ALTER EGOS AND GUIDE THEM THROUGH A VIRTUAL WORLD,

GRADUALLY UPGRADING ABILITIES AS THEY BATTLE MONSTERS AND GATHER LOOT.

THE GAME ALLOWS MISFITS TO BECOME MYTHIC SUPERHEROES,

AND FACE EPIC ADVENTURES AND HARROWING CHALLENGES.

IT'S WRITTEN IN EVERY MAN'S HEART.

WE WANT TO FEEL LIKE WARRIORS.

THAT'S WHAT GRAMPS LET PEOPLE DO.

MOST ASPECTS OF D&D CAN BE EXPRESSED NUMERICALLY—

ATTRIBUTES LIKE STRENGTH,

HEALTH,

AND INTELLIGENCE,

OR THE POWER OF A WEAPON,

THE PROBABILITY THAT IT WILL SUCCESSFULLY CONNECT WITH AN ENEMY,

AND THE AMOUNT OF DAMAGE IT WILL INFLICT.

BUT ONE PLAYER HAS TO PAINT A PICTURE WITH WORDS.

THAT PERSON ASSUMES THE ROLE OF THE DUNGEON MASTER.

THE DUNGEON MASTER DESCRIBES FOR OTHER PLAYERS WHAT THEY SEE AND HEAR IN THIS IMAGINARY WORLD, AND WHAT EFFECTS THEIR ACTIONS HAVE.

THE GAME IS PLAYED PRIMARILY IN YOUR HEAD.

THE ONLY OTHER THING YOU NEED IS A DIE TO DETERMINE PROBABILITY.

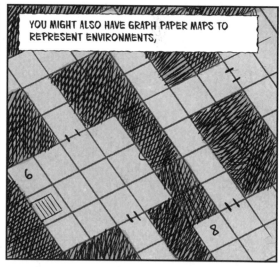

YOU MIGHT ALSO HAVE GRAPH PAPER MAPS TO REPRESENT ENVIRONMENTS,

FIGURINES TO REPRESENT YOUR CHARACTERS,

AND A FEW D&D RULE BOOKS FOR REFERENCE.

GYGAX FORGED AN INDUSTRY AROUND D&D AND MADE A SMALL FORTUNE IN THE PROCESS.

HIS HOME-BREW PUBLISHING COMPANY, TACTICAL STUDIES RULES, WENT FROM A BASEMENT ENTERPRISE TO A THRIVING CORPORATION WITH 600 EMPLOYEES IN LESS THAN A DECADE.

D&D HAS SOLD OVER $1 BILLION IN BOOKS AND MERCHANDISE.

IT HAS BEEN PLAYED BY 20 MILLION PEOPLE,

AND TRANSLATED INTO MORE THAN A DOZEN LANGUAGES IN AT LEAST 50 COUNTRIES.

HIS CREATION BECAME A CORNERSTONE OF GEEK CULTURE—

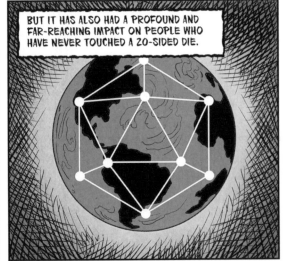

BUT IT HAS ALSO HAD A PROFOUND AND FAR-REACHING IMPACT ON PEOPLE WHO HAVE NEVER TOUCHED A 20-SIDED DIE.

NOW, THIS AFTERNOON AT HIS PARTY, GYGAX SLOWLY LUMBERS INTO HIS HOUSE TO FETCH A DIE OF HIS OWN.

IT IS TIME TO GET HIS GAME ON.

ARE YOU READY TO BEGIN?

CHAPTER TWO

YOU ARE ERNEST GARY GYGAX.

YOU WERE BORN IN CHICAGO ON JULY 27, 1938.

EVERY SUMMER, YOUR PARENTS DRIVE YOU TO YOUR GRANDPARENTS' HOME 80 MILES AWAY,

IN THE SMALL, SCENIC TOURIST TOWN OF LAKE GENEVA, WISCONSIN.

YOUR MOTHER, EMELIE, WAS BORN HERE, WHERE HER FAMILY HAS LIVED SINCE 1838.

YOU MOVE THERE IN 1946, JUST BEFORE YOUR EIGHTH BIRTHDAY.

YOU ARE SKILLED IN HUNTING,

WHETHER TAKING OUT SQUIRRELS WITH A .22

OR SHOOTING WILD PHEASANTS WITH A 16-GAUGE SHOTGUN.

YOU ARE NOT A LONER OR A GEEK.

YOU PLAY BASEBALL AND FOOTBALL WITH YOUR FRIENDS.

YOU ENJOY THE SMALL-TOWN FEEL.

YOU AND YOUR BUDDIES BEFRIEND THE LOCAL COBBLER,

WHO GIVES YOU PIECES OF LEATHER WITH WHICH YOU FASHION SLINGS.

IF YOUR BASEBALL BAT BREAKS, THE COBBLER FIXES IT FOR YOU WITH HIS SHOE REPAIR GLUE.

YOU ENJOY WATCHING HIM WORK.

YOUR FATHER, ERNEST, WAS BORN IN SWITZERLAND.

HE IS A SUIT SALESMAN AND ONE-TIME VIOLINIST FOR THE CHICAGO SYMPHONY ORCHESTRA.

HE MAKES UP BEDTIME STORIES FOR YOU,

FANTASTICAL YARNS ABOUT HEROES WITH MAGIC RINGS AND INVISIBILITY CLOAKS.

HE WAS AN EXCELLENT STORYTELLER.

YOUR MOTHER ALSO FILLS YOUR IMAGINATION WITH ADVENTURE.

SHE READS YOU TOM SAWYER AND HUCK FINN.

"WE STAYED IN THE WIGWAM AND LET THE RAFT TAKE CARE OF ITSELF."

"WHEN THE LIGHTNING GLARED OUT WE COULD SEE A BIG STRAIGHT RIVER AHEAD, AND HIGH, ROCKY BLUFFS ON BOTH SIDES."

IT'S A WEEKDAY MORNING IN THE EARLY 1950s.

BUS STOP

SIGH.

YOU CAN CHOOSE TO GO TO SCHOOL AND MAX OUT YOUR GRADE POINT AVERAGE—

OR GO EXPLORE THE SEPULCHRAL SYSTEM OF TUNNELS UNDERNEATH THE OLD OAK HILL SANITARIUM

OR AN ABANDONED INSANE ASYLUM NEAR THE LAKE.

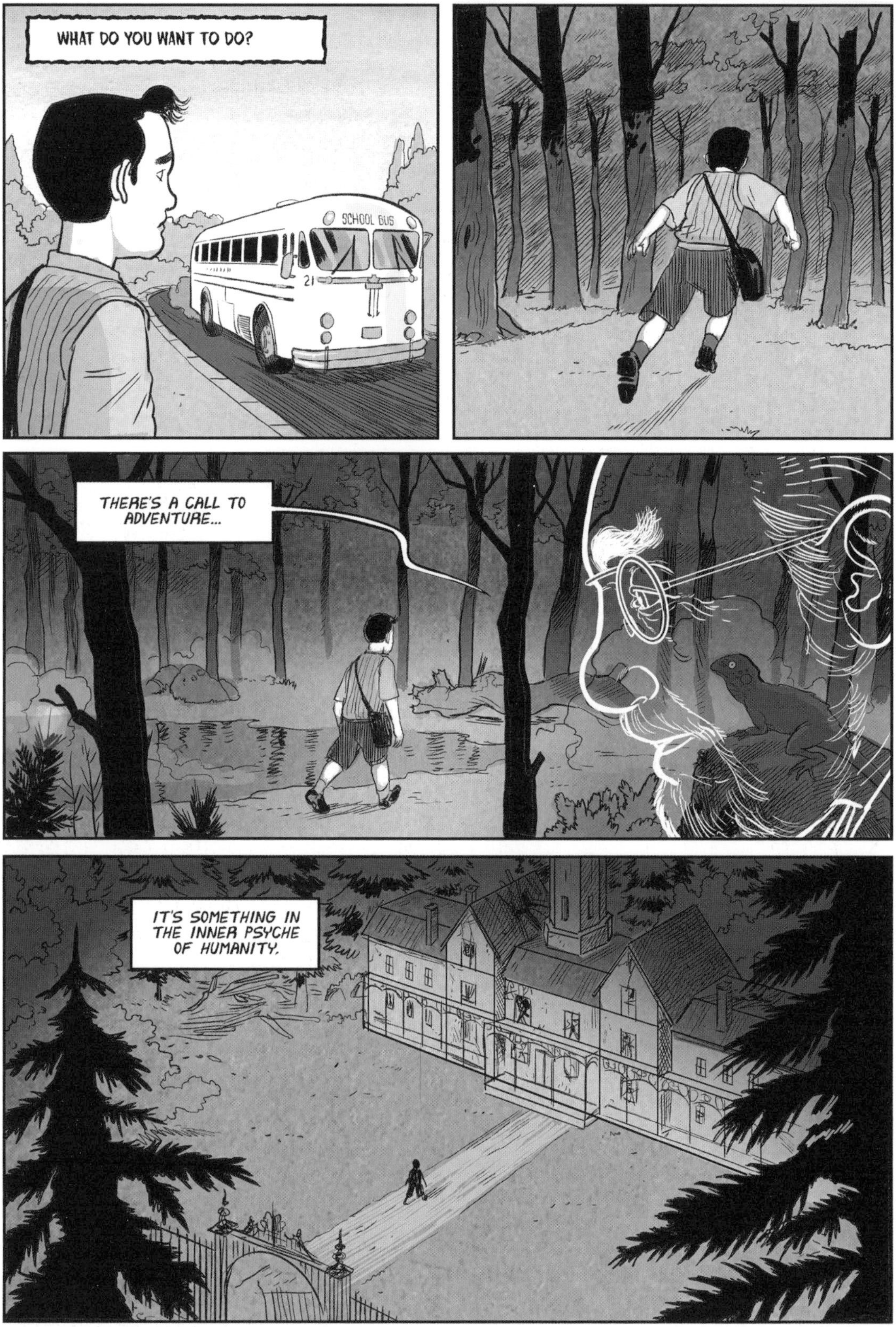
WHAT DO YOU WANT TO DO?
SCHOOL BUS
21
THERE'S A CALL TO ADVENTURE...
IT'S SOMETHING IN THE INNER PSYCHE OF HUMANITY.

YOU HAD TO WATCH OUT.

STRANGE LOCALS HUNG OUT IN THE EMPTY TUNNELS.

BANG!

ONE OF THEM SHOOTS AT YOU WITH A PELLET GUN!

POP!

ANOTHER, A BIG GUY, LIKES TO HARASS YOU AND YOUR FRIENDS.

YOU ARE BRIGHT, BUT TUNNEL-CRAWLING HOLDS A LOT MORE APPEAL THAN GRINDING AWAY IN THE CLASSROOM.

I HATED SCHOOL, DIDN'T LIKE THE DISCIPLINE.

GYGAX!

IN FIFTH GRADE, I MUST HAVE SPENT A MONTH IN DETENTION.

I CAN REMEMBER SITTING IN THE CLASSROOM.

TICK TOCK, TICK TOCK...

YOU DROP OUT IN JUNIOR YEAR.

YOU DRIFT A BIT AFTER HIGH SCHOOL, WORKING ODD JOBS DURING THE DAY.

YOU BAG GROCERIES—

WASH DISHES—

WORK AS A THEATER USHER—

RIIIIIP!

STOCK BEER AT A BAR.

YOU WORK WITH YOUR COUSIN REPAIRING AND SELLING PIPE ORGANS, BUT YOU LAMENT THAT YOU HAVEN'T GOT A GREAT EAR FOR IT.

DING!

I CAN'T CARRY A TUNE IN A BUSHEL BASKET!

YOU FIND YOURSELF MORE ADEPT AT PLAYING GAMES.

IN YOUR SPARE TIME, YOU ENJOY PINOCHLE AND CHESS—BUT YOU AREN'T THAT GOOD.

CHECKMATE.

I NEVER DID PLAY PARTICULARLY WELL.

BY 18, YOU MOVE BACK TO CHICAGO...

AND YOU DISCOVER A NEW DIVERSION THAT CHANGES YOUR LIFE—

WAR GAMES!

24

MANY TRACE THE ORIGIN OF WAR GAMES TO A 1913 WORK BY H. G. WELLS...

LITTLE WARS

H. G. WELLS

IT WAS TITLED "LITTLE WARS: A GAME FOR BOYS FROM TWELVE YEARS OF AGE TO ONE HUNDRED AND FIFTY AND FOR THAT MORE INTELLIGENT SORT OF GIRL WHO LIKES BOYS' GAMES AND BOOKS."

IN THIS 60-PAGE BOOK, WELLS DESCRIBES HOW HE AND A FRIEND COMMANDEERED HIS SON'S TOY SOLDIERS AND MADE UP A GAME OF THEIR OWN.

THEY SITUATED THE TOY SOLDIERS ON AN IMAGINARY BATTLEFIELD AND TOOK TURNS MANEUVERING THEM FOR TACTICAL ADVANTAGE.

WELLS WROTE ABOUT THE MANY ITERATIONS HE'D GONE THROUGH WHILE PERFECTING THE RULES.

HE LAID THEM OUT IN GREAT DETAIL SO THAT READERS COULD PLAY THE GAME THEMSELVES.

YOU AND YOUR FRIENDS WOULD BUILD DETAILED TABLETOP RECREATIONS OF FAMOUS BATTLEFIELDS—SAY, GETTYSBURG.

YOU POSITION TOYS REPRESENTING BATTALIONS OF INFANTRY, CAVALRY, AND ARTILLERY EMPLACEMENTS.

ARMED WITH RULERS AND PROTRACTORS, YOU TAKE TURNS MOVING YOUR UNITS IN CAREFULLY MEASURED INCREMENTS.

SKIRMISHES GET RESOLVED BY A ROLL OF THE DICE.

ONE PLAYER SERVES AS REFEREE AND JUDGE, SETTLING DISPUTES OVER THE FINER POINTS OF RULES AND HISTORICAL ACCURACY.

YOU MARRY IN 1958, AT AGE 20,

AND HAVE TWO CHILDREN BY 1961.

BUT YOU CONTINUE TO SPEND MUCH OF YOUR FREE TIME LOCKED IN EPIC IMAGINARY BATTLES, SOME OF WHICH LAST FOR MONTHS.

YOU ALSO PLAY BY MAIL WITH OTHER WAR GAMERS ACROSS THE COUNTRY.

YOU ARE FASCINATED BY THE WAY THE ROLLING OF DICE AFFECTS—AND ENLIVENS— THE GAME EXPERIENCE.

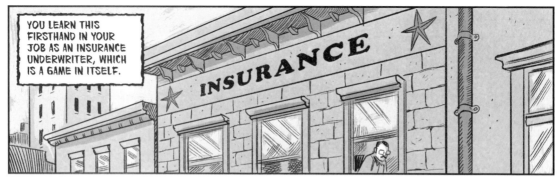

YOU LEARN THIS FIRSTHAND IN YOUR JOB AS AN INSURANCE UNDERWRITER, WHICH IS A GAME IN ITSELF.

YOU EVALUATE POLICIES AND CALCULATE HOW MUCH TO CHARGE IN PREMIUMS BASED ON SALARY, AGE, MEDICAL REPORTS, AND THE POTENTIAL FOR LONG-TERM DISABILITIES.

YOU DO SPECIAL RISK UNDERWRITING,

SUCH AS EVALUATING THE PAYOUT FOR A MAJOR LEAGUE BASEBALL TEAM THAT WANTS TO TAKE OUT A POLICY ON ONE OF ITS PLAYERS.

I WASN'T POPULAR IN THE HOME OFFICE BECAUSE I WASN'T CHICKEN.

I'M JUST A RISK TAKER. I HAVE GUT INSTINCTS.

YOU TAKE SIMILAR LIBERTIES IN WAR GAMES.

YOU HAVE LITTLE TIME FOR PEOPLE WHO PLAY TOO MUCH BY-THE-BOOK.

BUT THAT'S AGAINST THE RULES, GARY.

THEN THE RULES NEED TO BE CHANGED.

YOU AND A FEW BUDDIES CARRY THIS DO-IT-YOURSELF SPIRIT EVEN FURTHER, DEVISING A GAME OF YOUR OWN AROUND WWII TANK COMBAT.

YOU'RE DETERMINED THAT YOUR GAME AVOID WHAT YOU CALL THE "GOOFY BELL CURVE" THAT RESULTS FROM ROLLING A PAIR OF SIX-SIDED DICE.

TWOS AND TWELVES ARE RARE;

SIXES, SEVENS, AND EIGHTS ARE COMPARATIVELY FREQUENT.

TO ACHIEVE A MORE LINEAR CURVE, YOU DETERMINE THAT PLAYERS

MUST PLUCK 1 OF 20 NUMBERED POKER CHIPS FROM A HAT.

THIS WAY THERE IS AN EQUAL 5 PERCENT PROBABILITY OF EACH OUTCOME.

LATER YOU FIND THE PERFECT REPLACEMENT FOR THIS CLUNKY SYSTEM.

IN A SCHOOL SUPPLY CATALOG, YOU DISCOVER DICE SHAPED LIKE ALL OF THE PLATONIC SOLIDS, INCLUDING THE ICOSAHEDRON—

$2.99

A 20-SIDED DIE.

AFTER MOVING BACK TO LAKE GENEVA, YOU BEGIN GAMING IN EARNEST IN YOUR BASEMENT.

YOU AND YOUR FELLOW GAMERS CALL YOURSELVES THE LAKE GENEVA TACTICAL STUDIES ASSOCIATION.

YOUR INVENTIVENESS AND ORGANIZATIONAL SKILLS LEAD YOU TO PUT TOGETHER THE FIRST LAKE GENEVA CONVENTION,

OR GENCON FOR SHORT.

GENCON

HORTICULTURAL HALL

YOU HOLD THE CONVENTION AT YOUR HOMETOWN'S VINE-COVERED HORTICULTURAL HALL IN 1968.

WANNABE GENERALS FROM ALL OVER THE US AND CANADA COME TO DO BATTLE.

EXIT

I COUGHED UP 50 BUCKS TO RENT THE HALL.

ADMISSION WAS $1, AND I WAS DELIGHTED BECAUSE I MADE JUST ENOUGH TO PAY MYSELF BACK.

GEN CON

$1.00

YOUR GROWING CIRCLE OF GAMER FRIENDS INTRODUCES YOU TO MANY TWEAKED AND MODIFIED VERSIONS OF EXISTING GAMES.

WE TWEAKED THIS ONE HERE, MORE LIKE OPERATION OVERLOAD.

THE ROOTS OF DUNGEONS & DRAGONS BEGAN ONE NIGHT IN 1968...

YOUR FRIEND JEFF PERREN BRINGS OVER SOME MINIATURES FROM A MEDIEVAL WAR GAME CALLED "SIEGE OF BODENBERG."

PERREN HAS FOUR PAGES OF RULES,

WHICH YOU EXPAND INTO AN ENTIRELY NEW GAME: 16 PAGES OF INSTRUCTIONS THAT YOU DUB "CHAINMAIL."

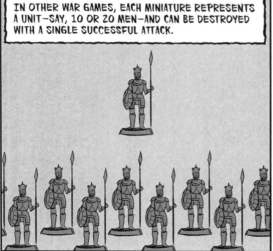

IN OTHER WAR GAMES, EACH MINIATURE REPRESENTS A UNIT—SAY, 10 OR 20 MEN—AND CAN BE DESTROYED WITH A SINGLE SUCCESSFUL ATTACK.

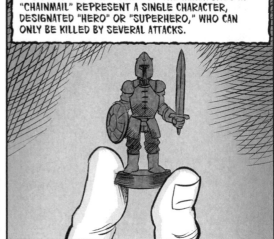

YOU DECIDE TO MAKE SOME OF THE MINIATURES IN "CHAINMAIL" REPRESENT A SINGLE CHARACTER, DESIGNATED "HERO" OR "SUPERHERO," WHO CAN ONLY BE KILLED BY SEVERAL ATTACKS.

FOR THE HELL OF IT, YOU INCLUDE A SUPPLEMENTAL SET OF RULES THAT FEATURES MAGICAL FANTASY TRAPPINGS:

DRAGONS—

ELVES—

WIZARDS—

FIREBALLS.

YOU'RE A FAN OF THE "CONAN THE BARBARIAN" BOOKS BY ROBERT E. HOWARD.

YOU HOPE TO EVOKE THEIR SWASHBUCKLING ACTION IN A WAR GAME.

BUT YOU LOATHE THE MAJOR FANTASY TOUCHSTONE OF THE TIME, J. R. R. TOLKIEN'S LORD OF THE RINGS SERIES.

IT WAS SO DULL.

I MEAN, THERE WAS NO ACTION IN IT.

I'D REALLY LIKE TO THROTTLE BILBO AND FRODO.

37

FEW OF THE HISTORY BUFF WAR GAMERS APPRECIATE HOW YOUR INNOVATIVE TWISTS PERSONALIZE THE PLAY EXPERIENCE.

SO INSTEAD OF A GENERAL, YOU'RE A WIZARD!

WHAT?

YOU CAN'T BE A WIZARD.

IT'S A GAME! YOU CAN BE ANYTHING!

IN THAT CASE—I CAN BE OUT OF HERE!

THEY CAN'T GET PAST THE MAGICAL ASPECTS, WHICH THEY VIEW AS FOLLY AT BEST, HERESY AT WORST.

YOU EKE OUT A LIVING AS A COBBLER, WORKING ON YOUR GAME IN YOUR SPARE TIME.

ONE DAY, YOU CATCH A BREAK THAT WILL CHANGE YOUR LIFE.

A FRIEND WHO HAD STARTED A SMALL GAME COMPANY OFFERS TO PUBLISH YOUR GAME, AND YOU AGREE.

I THINK YOU'RE ONTO SOMETHING HERE, GARY.

"CHAINMAIL: RULES FOR MEDIEVAL MINIATURES" IS RELEASED IN 1971 FOR $3 EACH.

IT SOON BECOMES THE PUBLISHER'S BIGGEST HIT YET, SELLING 100 COPIES A MONTH.

THOUGH THE GAME ISN'T MAKING YOU RICH, YOU WONDER IF DESIGNING GAMES MIGHT BECOME MORE THAN JUST A HOBBY.

MAYBE IT COULD BECOME A FULL-TIME JOB. MAYBE IT'S YOUR DESTINY!

BUT THE CREATION OF DUNGEONS & DRAGONS NEEDED ONE MORE PERSON TO BRING IT TO LIFE...

CHAPTER THREE

YOU ARE DAVE ARNESON.

YOU ARE 21 YEARS OLD.

IT IS 1969.

YOU ARE A PART-TIME SECURITY GUARD

AND A HISTORY STUDENT AT THE UNIVERSITY OF MINNESOTA.

YOU SPEND MOST OF YOUR SALARY BUYING SODAS FOR YOUR BUDDIES, WHO MEET TO PLAY GAMES IN YOUR PARENTS' BASEMENT.

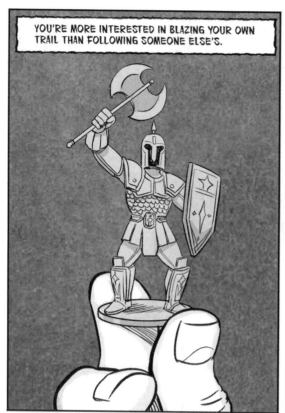

YOU'RE MORE INTERESTED IN BLAZING YOUR OWN TRAIL THAN FOLLOWING SOMEONE ELSE'S.

YOU HOLE UP IN THE SCHOOL LIBRARY, DOING EXHAUSTIVE RESEARCH TO MAKE YOUR WAR GAMES MORE ACCURATE.

IT RECENTLY OCCURRED TO YOU THAT YOU MIGHT GET BETTER GRADES IF YOU DIDN'T INTERRUPT YOUR TEACHERS TO ARGUE THE FINER POINTS OF HISTORY.

ACTUALLY, THE CONVOY APPROACHED ORLÉANS FROM THE NORTH, NOT FROM THE WEST.

YOU JOURNEY FROM THE TWIN CITIES TO ATTEND THE SECOND GENCON IN AUGUST 1969.

Welcome To LAKE GENEVA WISCONSIN

YOU MEET GARY GYGAX THERE, AND YOU CAN'T HELP BUT BE A BIT AWED.

GEN CON

YOU THINK HE'S ONE OF THE BIGGEST MOVERS AND SHAKERS IN THE WHOLE MIDWESTERN WAR-GAMING SCENE.

HE TELLS YOU HE'S TRYING TO CREATE A RULE SET AROUND NAVAL COMBAT DURING THE WAR OF 1812.

THIS IS SOMETHING I'VE BEEN TINKERING WITH.

HE'S VERY IMPRESSED THAT YOU CAN RATTLE OFF PRICES OF MUSKETS AND RATIONS AND FRIGATES DURING THAT ERA.

HE ASKS YOU TO COLLABORATE ON THE GAME WITH HIM.

HOW ABOUT IT?

DO YOU ACCEPT?

44

YOU MEET GYGAX AT HIS HOUSE IN LAKE GENEVA.

YOU ARE THE ONE WAR GAMER WHO GROKS THE IMPORTANCE OF "CHAINMAIL" RIGHT AWAY.

YOU AND GYGAX HAVE RECENTLY WORKED TOGETHER ON A SAILING WAR GAME.

ONCE YOU GET TO KNOW GYGAX, YOU THINK HE'S A BIT OF AN OBSESSIVE,

SHOULD WE HAVE A CHART FOR FLOODING PROBABILITY?

OVERLY CONCERNED WITH CODIFYING AND DOCUMENTING THINGS.

LET'S ADD THAT IN THERE.

EH... SURE.

GARY ADDED THIS REALLY LAME SECTION ABOUT SINGLE-SHIP ACTIONS TO OUR GAME, WHICH NOBODY EVER USES.

DAVE WASN'T MUCH OF A RISK TAKER, DIDN'T CUT SCHOOL, PROBABLY NEVER GOT INTO FISTICUFFS.

BUT YOUR COMMON LOVE OF GAMING OVERCOMES YOUR DIFFERENCES.

WHEN YOU SEE "CHAINMAIL," YOU'RE INTRIGUED BY ITS POTENTIAL FOR FREE-FORM, IMPROVISATORY PLAY.

IT'S SIMILAR TO THE GAME SCENARIOS THAT ONE OF YOUR GAME GROUPS IN THE TWIN CITIES HAS BEEN PLAYING.

WE DIDN'T HAVE VOLUMES OF RULES AND PEOPLE ARGUING ABOUT HISTORICAL ACCURACY.

IN ONE GAME, WE ALL ENDED UP CHASING A SOUTH AMERICAN DICTATOR AS HE WAS TRYING TO ESCAPE WITH HIS COMIC BOOK COLLECTION.

YOU MODIFY "CHAINMAIL" FOR YOUR OWN GROUP'S PURPOSES.

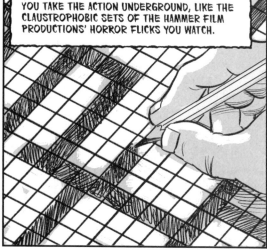

YOU TAKE THE ACTION UNDERGROUND, LIKE THE CLAUSTROPHOBIC SETS OF THE HAMMER FILM PRODUCTIONS' HORROR FLICKS YOU WATCH.

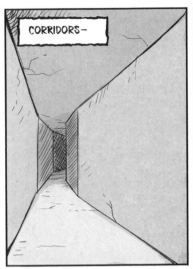

CORRIDORS—

TUNNELS—

CAVES!

A DUNGEON IS NICE AND SELF-CONTAINED.

PLAYERS CAN'T GO ROMPING OVER THE COUNTRYSIDE, AND YOU CAN CONTROL THE SITUATION.

YOU TEST YOUR "CHAINMAIL" MOD IN PLAY SESSIONS WITH YOUR GROUP AND, BASED ON THEIR FEEDBACK, CONTINUE TO TINKER WITH THE RULES TO MAKE IT MORE FUN.

WE HAD TO CHANGE THE COMBAT SYSTEM BECAUSE WE ADDED MORE MONSTERS.

THEY WERE GETTING BIG AND GRUESOME.

THERE'S ANOTHER ASPECT OF THE GAME YOU WANT TO TWEAK: THE FACT THAT IT ENDS.

YOUR GROUP IS HAVING TOO MUCH FUN PLAYING THESE SPECIFIC ROLES TO WANT TO PART WITH THEM AFTER A SINGLE GAME.

OUTSIDE OF THE INDIVIDUAL SESSIONS, YOU CREATE AN EXPERIENCE SYSTEM FOR CHARACTERS.

A CHARACTER EARNS EXPERIENCE POINTS BASED ON HIS OR HER SUCCESS FROM GAME TO GAME.

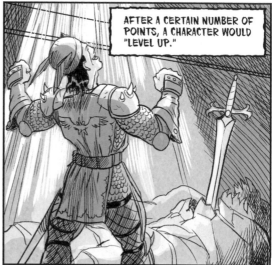

AFTER A CERTAIN NUMBER OF POINTS, A CHARACTER WOULD "LEVEL UP."

TO HELP MOVE THE STORY ALONG, YOU ASSUME A MORE ELABORATE ROLE THAN THAT OF THE REFEREES USED TO RESOLVE DISPUTES IN WAR GAMES.

YOU WOULD BE THE GAME MASTER— SETTING THE SCENE, GUIDING PLAYERS ALONG THEIR QUESTS.

YOU DEVELOP THE GAME FOR ABOUT SIX MONTHS WITH YOUR GROUP IN MINNESOTA...

THEN YOU AND A COUPLE OF YOUR BUDDIES TREK BACK TO LAKE GENEVA IN LATE 1971 TO RUN A GAME FOR GYGAX AND HIS CREW.

NO ONE KNOWS HOW ANCIENT THIS DUNGEON IS, OR HOW DEEP.

IT HOLDS MANY PERILS AS WELL AS TREASURES.

ALL YOU HEAR IS THE SOUND OF YOUR OWN FOOTSTEPS IN THE DARKNESS...

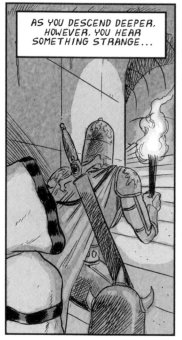

AS YOU DESCEND DEEPER, HOWEVER, YOU HEAR SOMETHING STRANGE...

YOU RUN INTO A TROLL WITH MAGIC ARMOR.

51

WE FOUGHT HIM, KILLED HIM, AND TOOK HIS TREASURE.

THE GAME SESSION ENDS AT MIDNIGHT.

THE WISCONSINITES LOVE IT!

YOU HAVE SUCCESSFULLY DISTILLED THE INVOLVED, TACTICAL MILITARY CAMPAIGNS INTO A VIRTUAL WORLD OF FIRST-PERSON ACTION.

GYGAX EFFUSES OVER WHAT HE CALLS THE "FUN HOUSE" ASPECT OF THE GAME.

IT REMINDS HIM OF EXPLORING THE TUNNELS UNDER THE INSANE ASYLUM AS A CHILD.

HE IMMEDIATELY SEES THE COMMERCIAL POTENTIAL IN THIS VARIANT OF "CHAINMAIL."

THIS IS IT— THE REAL DEAL, DAVE!

I THINK WE CAN MAKE SOMETHING SPECIAL OUT OF THIS.

YOU SOON AGREE TO COLLABORATE AGAIN.

BACK AT HOME, YOU RUN OFF A COPY OF YOUR NOTES ON YOUR DAD'S XEROX MACHINE AND MAIL THEM TO GYGAX,

WHO LATER SAYS HE "COULDN'T MAKE HEADS OR TAILS" OF THE "GENERALLY USELESS" NOTES.

GARY SENT ME A COUPLE OF DRAFTS TO LOOK OVER, AND WE TALKED ON THE PHONE A LOT.

YOU SHOULD SEE THE PHONE BILLS WE RAN UP.

DAVE!!!

GYGAX PUTS YOUR NOTES INTO A COHESIVE SET OF RULES.

HE COULD TYPE, AND I COULDN'T.

YOU HAVE WHAT COULD GENEROUSLY BE CALLED PHILOSOPHICAL DIFFERENCES WITH GYGAX.

HE THINKS YOU CAN WRITE A RULE TO COVER ANY SITUATION.

I DON'T.

THERE ARE JUST TOO MANY POSSIBILITIES.

ESPECIALLY WHEN YOU'RE ASKING PEOPLE TO USE THEIR IMAGINATIONS!

CHAPTER FOUR

YOU ARE GARY GYGAX.

YOU ARE AT HOME IN LAKE GENEVA, WISCONSIN,

BUSY CREATING THE GAME THAT WILL BECOME YOUR GREATEST LEGACY:

DUNGEONS & DRAGONS.

YOU BREAK THE CHARACTERS DOWN INTO A VARIETY OF CLASSES—

WIZARDS

WARRIORS

CLERICS

ROGUES

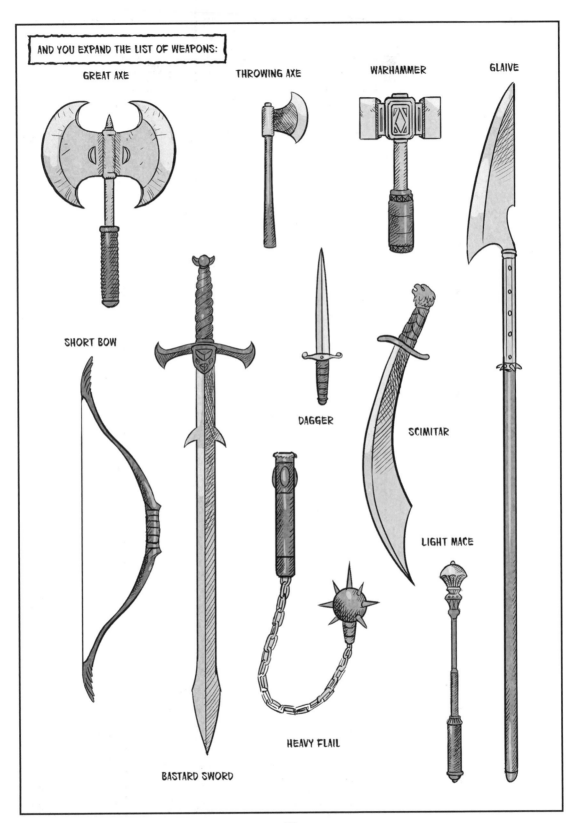

AND YOU EXPAND THE LIST OF WEAPONS:

GREAT AXE

THROWING AXE

WARHAMMER

GLAIVE

SHORT BOW

DAGGER

SCIMITAR

LIGHT MACE

HEAVY FLAIL

BASTARD SWORD

ONCE YOU HAVE A NEAR-FINAL SET OF RULES, YOU GO INTO YOUR STUDY, A SMALL ROOM OFF YOUR KITCHEN.

YOU PLACE AN 8-1/2-BY-11-INCH SHEET OF GRAPH PAPER ON YOUR DESK.

YOU BEGIN SKETCHING OUT A DUNGEON.

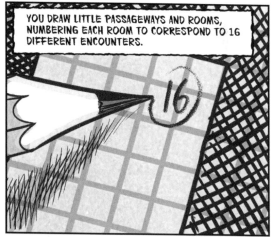

YOU DRAW LITTLE PASSAGEWAYS AND ROOMS, NUMBERING EACH ROOM TO CORRESPOND TO 16 DIFFERENT ENCOUNTERS.

DESIGNING THE GAME IS LIKE BUILDING A HAUNTED MANSION AND SETTING TRAPS WITH MONSTERS AND TREASURE.

WHEN YOU'RE THROUGH DEVELOPING YOUR GAME THAT NIGHT, YOU ASSEMBLE YOUR OWN TEAM OF TESTERS.

YOUR FRIEND DON KAYE;

TWO OF YOUR CHILDREN: 11-YEAR-OLD ERNIE

AND 9-YEAR-OLD ELISE;

AND A KID FROM UP THE STREET.

SNIFF!

60

YOU PLAY AROUND A TABLE.

FIRST YOU MAKE YOUR CHARACTERS.

I'LL BE A WARRIOR!

I'M AN ELF!

UM, CAN I BE THE WIZARD?

YOU GOT IT!

YOU HAND OUT INDEX CARDS THAT LIST SIX ATTRIBUTES ON EACH:

STRENGTH

INTELLIGENCE

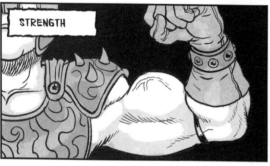

WISDOM

CONSTITUTION

DEXTERITY

CHARISMA

61

EACH PLAYER ROLLS THREE SIX-SIDED DICE TO GENERATE A VALUE FOR EACH CHARACTER ATTRIBUTE.

THE HIGHER THE INTELLIGENCE, FOR EXAMPLE, THE BETTER SPELLS A WIZARD COULD CAST.

THE HIGHER THE DEXTERITY, SAY, THE SHREWDER THE THIEF.

IT HELPED THE PERSON TO GET INTO THE ROLE THAT THEY WERE PLAYING.

IF THEY HAD A REAL LOW INTELLIGENCE THEY COULD PLAY IT LIKE, "DUH, OK."

ONCE THE PLAYERS FORM THEIR CHARACTERS, YOU PLAY THE ROLE OF DUNGEON MASTER.

THERE IS A RUINED CASTLE THAT YOU HAVE HEARD OF.

IT IS FILLED WITH STRANGE MONSTERS AND TREASURES, AND YOU WANT TO GET THEM.

YOUR OBJECT IS TO SLAY THE MONSTERS AND TAKE THEIR TREASURES AND BECOME MORE POWERFUL.

GO!

THE PLAYERS MAKE CHOICES —GO EAST, OPEN A DOOR— AND YOU RIFF ON WHAT HAPPENS.

WHEN THINGS GET SLOW, YOU SPEAK UP.

WHY ARE YOU STANDING IN THIS DEAD END?

TRYING TO LOOK FOR A SECRET DOOR?

YOU ROLL THE DICE TO DETERMINE THEIR FATE.

A SUCCESFUL ROLL OPENS A SECRET PASSAGE...

A HORDE OF ORCS TAKES YOU BY SURPRISE!

THEY HAVE YOU CORNERED!

WHAT WILL YOU DO?

YOU WATCH WITH DELIGHT AS A NEW FORM OF ENTERTAINMENT COMES INTO BEING.

YOU AREN'T SIMPLY GUIDING THE OTHER PLAYERS— YOU'RE A PARTICIPANT AS WELL, WATCHING IT UNFOLD AND GOING IN DIRECTIONS YOU NEVER ANTICIPATED.

ROLE-PLAYING ISN'T STORYTELLING.

IF THE DUNGEON MASTER IS DIRECTING IT, IT'S NOT A GAME.

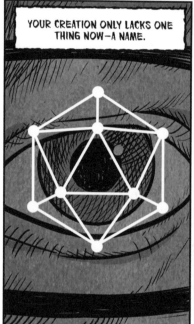

YOUR CREATION ONLY LACKS ONE THING NOW—A NAME.

HOW ABOUT... FANTASY & ADVENTURE.

SWORDS & SORCERY?

THAT SOUNDS CORNY.

HOW ABOUT DUNGEONS & DRAGONS?

OH DADDY!

I LIKE THAT ONE THE BEST!

65

YOU TAKE D&D TO AVALON HILL, THE BIGGEST WAR GAME PUBLISHER IN THE BUSINESS.

AND THE CHARACTERS LEVEL UP AND BECOME MORE POWERFUL OVER TIME.

SEE, THE GAME NEVER REALLY ENDS!

I THINK WE CAN SELL 50,000 COPIES OF IT.

IT'S GOING TO BE A HUGE HIT!

NO THANKS.

THEY COULDN'T UNDERSTAND A GAME WITH NO WINNERS AND LOSERS THAT JUST WENT ON AND ON.

IT'S 1973. YOU AND YOUR CHILDHOOD BUDDY DON KAYE ARE TALKING BUSINESS AT A LAKE GENEVA RESTAURANT.

WE HAVE NO MONEY, ZERO MANPOWER, AND NO INTEREST FROM GAME PUBLISHERS.

SO WHAT DO YOU SAY?

I'M IN!

YOU DECIDE TO FORM A COMPANY CALLED TACTICAL STUDIES RULES, OR TSR.

YOU DON'T ASK ARNESON TO JOIN.

DAVE WAS NEVER CONSIDERED AS A PARTNER.

WE DIDN'T FIGURE HE WAS THE KIND OF GUY WHO WOULD BE TOO GOOD AT RUNNING A BUSINESS.

GARY WAS WILLING TO GO AND MAKE THE PITCHES...

I WAS HAVING FUN!

THE D&D RULES YOU WRITE GROW FROM 50 PAGES TO 150 PAGES.

TSR SCRAPES TOGETHER $2,400 FOR START-UP COSTS.

IN JANUARY 1974, YOUR COMPANY RUNS OFF A THOUSAND COPIES OF THE BOOKLET, TITLED "DUNGEONS & DRAGONS: RULES FOR FANTASTIC MEDIEVAL WARGAMES CAMPAIGNS PLAYABLE WITH PAPER AND PENCIL AND MINIATURE FIGURES."

THE BOOKLET COSTS $10.

DUNGEONS & DRAGONS™

Rules for Fantastic Medieval Wargames Campaigns Playable with Paper and Pencil and Miniature Figures

GYGAX & ARNESON

3-VOLUME SET

PUBLISHED BY
TACTICAL STUDIES RULES
Price $10.00

THE EXTRA DICE NEEDED TO PLAY THE GAME ARE $3.50 EXTRA.

THE BASE OF OPERATIONS IS YOUR BASEMENT.

WOULD SOMEONE PROOFREAD THIS?

THEY NEVER DO PROOFREAD IT, THOUGH.

THERE ISN'T A MARKETING BUDGET.

D&D WILL LIVE AND DIE BY WORD OF MOUTH.

IT SPREADS FROM COLLEGE TO COLLEGE—

HOBBY SHOP TO HOBBY SHOP—

SCHOOLYARD TO SCHOOLYARD.

TEN MONTHS AFTER D&D'S LAUNCH, THE GAME SELLS OUT.

YOU PRINT TWICE AS MANY COPIES TO KEEP UP WITH DEMAND.

SOON YOUR SUPPLY RUNS OUT AGAIN.

TO FILL ORDERS, YOU WIPE MOLD OFF THE LAST FEW COPIES IN YOUR MUSTY CELLAR

PLAYERS CALL YOUR HOUSE AT ALL HOURS OF THE NIGHT...

RRRRRING!

HELLO?

MR. GYGAX? THIS IS PHIL RICHMOND, FROM FLAGSTAFF. ME AND MY FRIENDS HERE WERE WONDERING WHAT'S THE EXACT VOLUME OF SPACE COVERED BY THE "POWER WORD STUN" SPELL?

BING!

HELLO?

HELLO, IS THIS GARY GYGAX? I WAS WONDERING IF YOU HAD A FEW FREE HOURS TO ACT AS MY DUNGEON MASTER OVER THE PHONE.

YOU MAKE PROFITABLE UPGRADES TO THE GAME'S OPERATING SYSTEM.

"THE ADVANCED D&D PLAYER'S HANDBOOK" SOON APPEARS.

AD&D

YOU ALSO WRITE AND PUBLISH THE "MONSTER MANUAL,"

WHICH GIVES DESCRIPTIONS AND NUMERICAL ATTRIBUTES OF THE MANY DIFFERENT KINDS OF FOUL CREATURES THAT PLAYERS MIGHT FACE.

TSR ALSO SELLS THE EQUIVALENT OF SOFTWARE.

FOR ABOUT $5, A PLAYER CAN BUY PREPACKAGED CAMPAIGNS AND SCENARIOS BY YOU, ARNESON, OR OTHER SCRIBES OF THE TABLETOP GAMING INDUSTRY.

2 MODULES

ADVANCED DUNGEONS & DRAGONS™

Dungeon Module T1
The Village of Hommlet

by Gary Gygax

INTRODUCTORY TO NOVICE LEVEL

The Village of Hommlet has grown up around a crossroads in a woodland. Once far from any important activity, it became embroiled in the struggle between gods and demons when the Temple of Elemental Evil arose but a few leagues away. Luckily for its inhabitants, the Temple and its evil hordes were destroyed a decade ago, but Hommlet still suffers from incursions of bandits and strange monsters.

This module contains a map of the village and lands around, a large scale map of the inn, church, trading post, and guard tower (main floor, upper rooms and cellars), an informational key regarding the inhabitants, and a map and exploration key for a destroyed moat house, a former outpost of the Temple of Elemental Evil. The whole provides a complete, ready-to-play scenario, and is a lead-in to DUNGEON MODULE T2, THE TEMPLE OF ELEMENTAL EVIL.

ANYONE CAN BUILD INDIVIDUAL "APPLICATIONS" THAT RUN ON TOP OF THE RULES.

CHAPTER FIVE

YOU ARE DAVE ARNESON, TEACHING STUDENTS ABOUT THE HISTORY OF DUNGEONS & DRAGONS.

YOU TAKE OUT A PILE OF COLORFUL BOOKLETS FROM YOUR BRIEFCASE.

Dungeon Module U2
Danger at Dunwater

THE MODULES WERE EVEN MORE PROFITABLE THAN THE RULES WERE.

MODULES

DID D&D HAVE ANY EFFECT ON THE CONVENTIONS?

THE WHOLE TENOR OF THE CROWD CHANGED.

WAR GAMERS SAT AROUND TALKING ABOUT THE LATEST HISTORICAL BOOKS...

BUT THESE D&D GUYS WERE FROM THE SCIENCE FICTION COMMUNITY.

AND THERE WERE WOMEN!

YOU GO FROM HAVING NONE AT A CONVENTION TO HAVING—WHOO!— 20 PERCENT WOMEN!

NO GROUPIES THOUGH, DARN IT.

YOU AND GYGAX BECOME FOLK HEROES AND, AT TIMES, TARGETS.

DAVE ARNESON! WOULD YOU HAVE TIME TO JOIN ME FOR A SHORT GAME?

SURE!

A PSUEDO FAN LURES YOU INTO A TRAP.

OK LET'S ROLL THE DICE AND SEE WHAT HAPPENS.

IT LOOKS LIKE THE BLOW FROM THE GRIFFON WAS FATAL.

YOUR ARMOR FAILS. YOU DIE.

THE GREAT DAVE ARNESON, BEAT AFTER ONLY ONE HOUR!

HE SPENT THE REST OF THE CONVENTION TELLING EVERYONE HOW HIS DUNGEON HAD KILLED ME.

HE'S LUCKY I DIDN'T FIND HIM IN A DARK STAIRWELL. WE WOULD HAVE SEEN WHO'D KILL WHO!

ACROSS THE CONTINENT, IN THE MASSACHUSETTS INSTITUTE OF TECHNOLOGY, A GROUP OF COLLEGE KIDS MONKEYING AROUND ON ENORMOUS MAINFRAME COMPUTERS FIND THEMSELVES DRAWN TO THE FAMILIAR SYSTEMS OF THE GAME.

ONE OF THEM IS WILL CROWTHER.

CROWTHER IS INTO FANTASY ROLE-PLAYING GAMES,

AND SPELUNKING.

IN 1976, HE COMBINES HIS INTERESTS TO CREATE THE FIRST TEXT-BASED ADVENTURE GAME.

IT'S CALLED "COLOSSAL CAVE ADVENTURE."

BY TYPING IN A DIRECTION, SUCH AS "NORTH" OR "SOUTH," OR A COMMAND, AS IN "HIT" OR "ATTACK," PLAYERS CAN BATTLE ENEMIES AND HUNT FOR TREASURE.

BEFORE LONG, STUDENTS AND HACKERS IN COMPUTER LABS ACROSS THE COUNTRY ARE PLAYING AND MODIFYING THE GAME'S CODE.

DON WOODS, A STANFORD STUDENT, CREATES A SPIN-OFF WITH CROWTHER'S BLESSING.

IT ADDED AUTOMATED MODERATION SO YOU DIDN'T NEED A HUMAN GAME MASTER.

IN 1978, STUDENTS AT THE UNIVERSITY OF ESSEX IN ENGLAND PIONEER A WAY TO EMULATE THE MULTI-PLAYER EXPERIENCE OF D&D ACROSS THE ADVANCED RESEARCH PROJECTS AGENCY NETWORK—

ALSO KNOWN AS ARPANET.

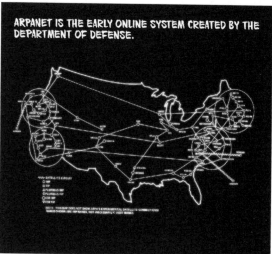

ARPANET IS THE EARLY ONLINE SYSTEM CREATED BY THE DEPARTMENT OF DEFENSE.

RICHARD BARTLE CODES THE FIRST MULTIUSER DUNGEON, OR MUD FOR SHORT.

A MUD IS A TEXT-BASED GAME WITH D&D MECHANICS OF EXPERIENCE POINTS AND LEVELS, AND AN EMPHASIS ON SOCIALIZATION AND CHATTING.

MUD WAS JUST A CONTINUATION OF WHAT I WAS DOING IN D&D.

81

RICHARD "LORD BRITISH" GARRIOTT ENCOUNTERS THE GAME AT COMPUTER CAMP IN 1977.

BACK HOME HE ORGANIZES D&D SESSIONS WITH HIS FRIENDS,

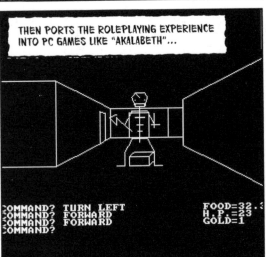

THEN PORTS THE ROLEPLAYING EXPERIENCE INTO PC GAMES LIKE "AKALABETH"...

AND LATER THE "ULTIMA" FRANCHISE.

HE SAYS THAT D&D'S PRIMORDIAL GAME ENGINE IS A PERFECT MATCH FOR NUMBER-CRUNCHING HOME COMPUTERS.

D&D ALLOWED PEOPLE TO BUILD A NUMERICAL REPRESENTATION OF THEMSELVES.

A NUMERICAL REPRESENTATION OF A MONSTER...

A NUMERICAL REPRESENTATION OF HOW A CHARACTER AND MONSTERS COULD INTERACT...

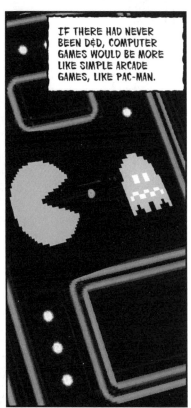

IF THERE HAD NEVER BEEN D&D, COMPUTER GAMES WOULD BE MORE LIKE SIMPLE ARCADE GAMES, LIKE PAC-MAN.

THE GAME'S INFLUENCE IS EXPANDING,

BUT NOT ALWAYS IN THE BEST WAYS...

CHAPTER SIX

YOU ARE WILLIAM DEAR, A SUCCESSFUL PRIVATE INVESTIGATOR FROM DALLAS.

YOU ARE A SWASHBUCKLING, BURT REYNOLDS-STYLE 1970s TOUGH GUY.

YOU LOVE TO HUNT.

YOU LIVE ON AN OSTENTATIOUS RANCH.

YOU POSE FOR PICTURES CLUTCHING YOUR FAVORITE WEAPON, A MACHINE GUN.

BUT YOU ARE AMONG THE BEST AT CRACKING MISSING PERSONS' CASES,

CREEK MISSING FOUND

CASE SOLVED

LOST DAUGHTER

UNTIL THE ONE ABOUT A YOUNG DUNGEONS & DRAGONS PLAYER, JAMES DALLAS EGBERT III, COMES YOUR WAY.

I HAVE SOMEONE ON LINE ONE. THEY SAY IT'S URGENT.

PATCH THEM THROUGH.

ON AUGUST 15, 1979, EGBERT VANISHES FROM HIS COLLEGE, MICHIGAN STATE UNIVERSITY IN EAST LANSING, MICHIGAN.

A CHILD PRODIGY WHO IS A SOPHOMORE AT THE AGE OF 16, HE LEAVES BEHIND CLUES AS CRYPTIC AS THE GAME HE MOST ENJOYS TO PLAY.

IN HIS DORM ROOM IS A CORK BULLETIN BOARD COVERED WITH A SEEMINGLY MEANINGFUL ARRANGEMENT OF THUMBTACKS.

NEXT TO IT IS AN UNSIGNED NOTE REQUESTING THAT HIS BODY, IF FOUND, SHOULD BE CREMATED.

THE HANDWRITING DOES NOT MATCH EGBERT'S.

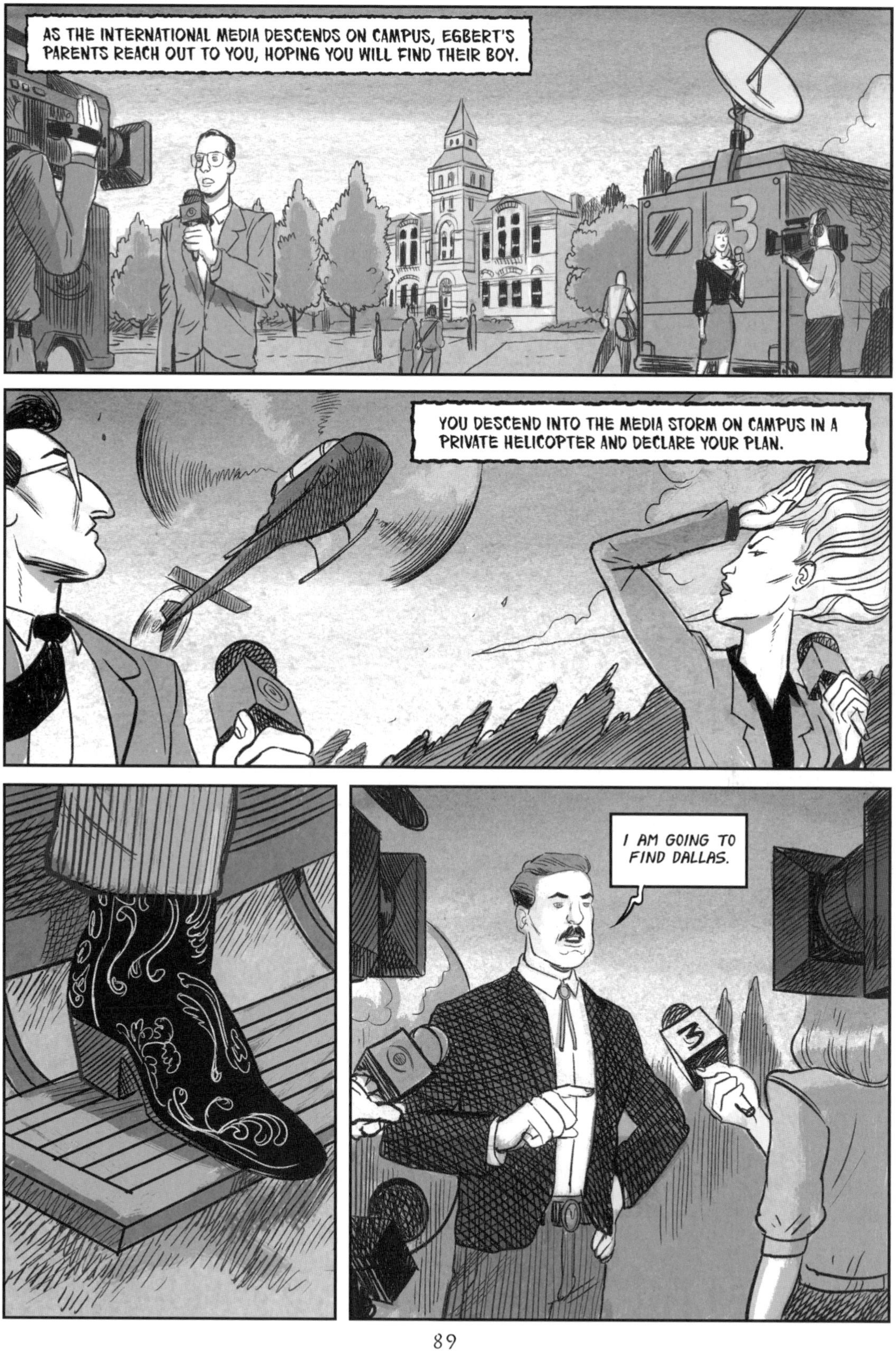
AS THE INTERNATIONAL MEDIA DESCENDS ON CAMPUS, EGBERT'S PARENTS REACH OUT TO YOU, HOPING YOU WILL FIND THEIR BOY.
YOU DESCEND INTO THE MEDIA STORM ON CAMPUS IN A PRIVATE HELICOPTER AND DECLARE YOUR PLAN.
I AM GOING TO FIND DALLAS.

THE PATH TO THE BOY, YOU BELIEVE, RESIDES SOMEWHERE INSIDE THIS DUNGEONS & DRAGONS GAME.

THE CHARACTER DALLAS CHOSE TO PLAY WAS HIMSELF.

STRENGTH AND CHARISMA HE DID NOT POSSESS, BUT INTELLIGENCE AND DEXTERITY, YES.

THE PRESS EAT IT UP.

STORIES HIT THE WIRES ABOUT THE BOY GENIUS WHO DISAPPEARED IN THE STEAM TUNNELS OF HIS UNIVERSITY WHILE ENACTING A REAL-LIFE VERSION OF D&D.

THE GAME, WHICH HAS BEEN A CULT PHENOMENON UP UNTIL THIS POINT, HITS POP CULTURE LIKE SOMETHING OUT OF THE SALEM WITCH TRIALS.

D&D D&D D&D D&D D&D D&D D&D D&D D&D

DEMONS!

INCANTATIONS!

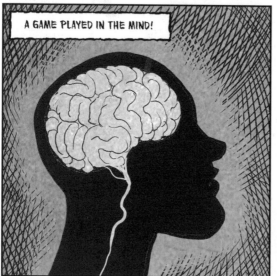

A GAME PLAYED IN THE MIND!

IT'S DIFFICULT TO GRASP, AND SEEMINGLY EVIL TO BEHOLD.

YOU WONDER: WHAT IS IT ABOUT THIS GAME THAT MIGHT HAVE CORRUPTED A GIFTED YOUNG MAN AND LED TO HIS APPARENT DEATH OR SUICIDE?

YOU GROW INCREASINGLY OBSESSIVE THROUGHOUT YOUR INVESTIGATION.

THE BOY, AS YOU FIND OUT, IS A TROUBLED SOUL.

HIS FRIENDS TELL YOU HE FELT DOMINATED BY HIS MOTHER, A DEMANDING WOMAN FOR WHOM NO GRADE EVER SEEMED HIGH ENOUGH.

SHE WAS REALLY HARD ON HIM.

EGBERT WAS ALSO TRYING TO HIDE THE FACT THAT HE WAS GAY FROM HIS PARENTS, AND HAD DESCENDED INTO DRUG AND ALCOHOL ABUSE.

YOU TAKE A D&D APPROACH TO SOLVING THE CASE, BY PUTTING YOURSELF INTO THE MIND OF EGBERT.

YOU'RE GOING TO GET INSIDE DALLAS'S HEAD.

YOU HIRE KIDS TO PLAY DUNGEONS & DRAGONS WITH YOU—

AND PLUMB THE STEAM TUNNELS YOURSELF.

YOU LEARN THAT EGBERT— AND MANY OTHER D&D PLAYERS ON CAMPUS— HAVE BEEN USING THE UNDERGROUND STEAM TUNNELS TO PLAY, PARTY, AND HAVE SEX.

BUT THE BOY IS NOWHERE TO BE FOUND.

THREE WEEKS LATER, YOU GET A PHONE CALL IN THE MIDDLE OF THE NIGHT.

RRRINNG!

IT IS EGBERT. HE IS IN A SMALL TOWN IN LOUISIANA.

PHONE

PHILLIPS 66

MR. DEAR? THIS IS DALLAS EGBERT.

DALLAS! WHERE ARE YOU?

CAN WE MEET? BUT YOU HAVE TO PROMISE NOT TO TELL ANYONE.

YOU AGREE TO TELL NO ONE, AND TRAVEL TO MEET THE BOY.

EGBERT GIVES YOU THE ADDRESS OF A DECREPIT HOTEL IN A BAD PART OF TOWN.

YOU FIND HIM HUDDLED IN THE CORNER OF THE HOTEL ROOM.

BREAKING DOWN, THE BOY TELLS YOU THE STORY OF HIS LIFE:

HIS DOMINEERING MOTHER,

HIS DEPRESSION,

HIS ANXIETY ABOUT COMING OUT TO HIS PARENTS.

95

EGBERT SAYS THAT HE HAD PLANNED TO KILL HIMSELF IN THE STEAM TUNNELS.

HE HAD WRITTEN THE NOTE HIMSELF BUT WITH HIS LEFT HAND TO THROW PEOPLE OFF HIS TRAIL.

HE DIDN'T HAVE THE NERVE TO GO THROUGH WITH THE ACT, HOWEVER,

AND SPENT WEEKS CRASHING ON FRIENDS' COUCHES.

FINALLY, HE HITCHED A RIDE DOWN SOUTH TO THIS SPOT.

YOU KEEP YOUR WORD, REFUSING REPORTERS' REQUESTS TO TELL THE STORY OF WHAT HAD HAPPENED TO EGBERT DURING THOSE WEEKS HE WAS MISSING.

YOU VISIT EGBERT AND HIS PARENTS ON A FEW OCCASIONS.

WITH A SON OF YOUR OWN AROUND THE SAME AGE, YOU HAVE TAKEN ON A FATHERLY RELATIONSHIP WITH EGBERT.

BUT EGBERT NEVER RECOVERED FROM HIS DEPRESSION.

A YEAR AFTER HE DISAPPEARED, HE KILLED HIMSELF.

FIVE YEARS AFTER EGBERT'S DEATH, YOU REVEAL THE FULL STORY OF EGBERT'S DEPRESSION AND DRUG ABUSE.

BUT THE PUBLIC AND THE PRESS HAS ALREADY MADE UP ITS MIND.

D&D IS TO BLAME!

THE GAME STARTS GETTING MAINSTREAM MEDIA ATTENTION—

BUT NOT THE KIND GYGAX AND ARNESON WANT.

DUNGEONS AND DRAGONS: Just harmless fun—or sorcery?

'Dungeons and Dragons' deadly

Groups Say Fantasy Game Responsible for Teen Suicide

PATRICIA PULLING, A MOTHER WHO CLAIMED THAT HER SON SHOT HIMSELF IN THE CHEST AS A RESULT OF A "CURSE" HE RECEIVED IN A D&D GAME, FOUNDS AN ORGANIZATION CALLED B.A.D.D. (BOTHERED ABOUT DUNGEONS & DRAGONS).

STOP D&D!

DUNGEONS & DRAGONS KILL!

EN NOT GA

MRS. PULLING, WHY DO YOU CONSIDER D&D SO DANGEROUS?

IT IS NOT LIKE MONOPOLY... IT IS ROLE-PLAYING, WHICH IS TYPICALLY USED FOR BEHAVIOR MODIFICATION.

IN 1982, A TV MOVIE CALLED "MAZES AND MONSTERS" STARS A 26-YEAR-OLD TOM HANKS AS AN OBSESSIVE GAMER UNABLE TO DISTINGUISH FANTASY FROM REALITY.

PARDU! DON'T JUMP!

I HAVE SPELLS, I'M GOING TO FLY!

YOU DON'T HAVE ENOUGH POINTS!

I'M THE MAZE CONTROLLER!

JACK CHICK, A PROLIFIC AUTHOR OF RELIGIOUS TRACTS, PUBLISHES A COMIC CALLED "DARK DUNGEONS."

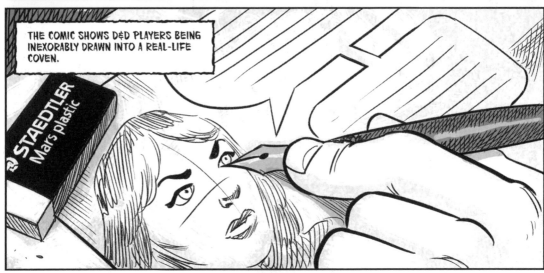

THE COMIC SHOWS D&D PLAYERS BEING INEXORABLY DRAWN INTO A REAL-LIFE COVEN.

Debbie, your cleric has been raised to the 8th level. I think it's time that you learn how to _really_ cast spells.

You mean you're going to teach me how to have _the real power?_

Yes, you have the personality for it, now

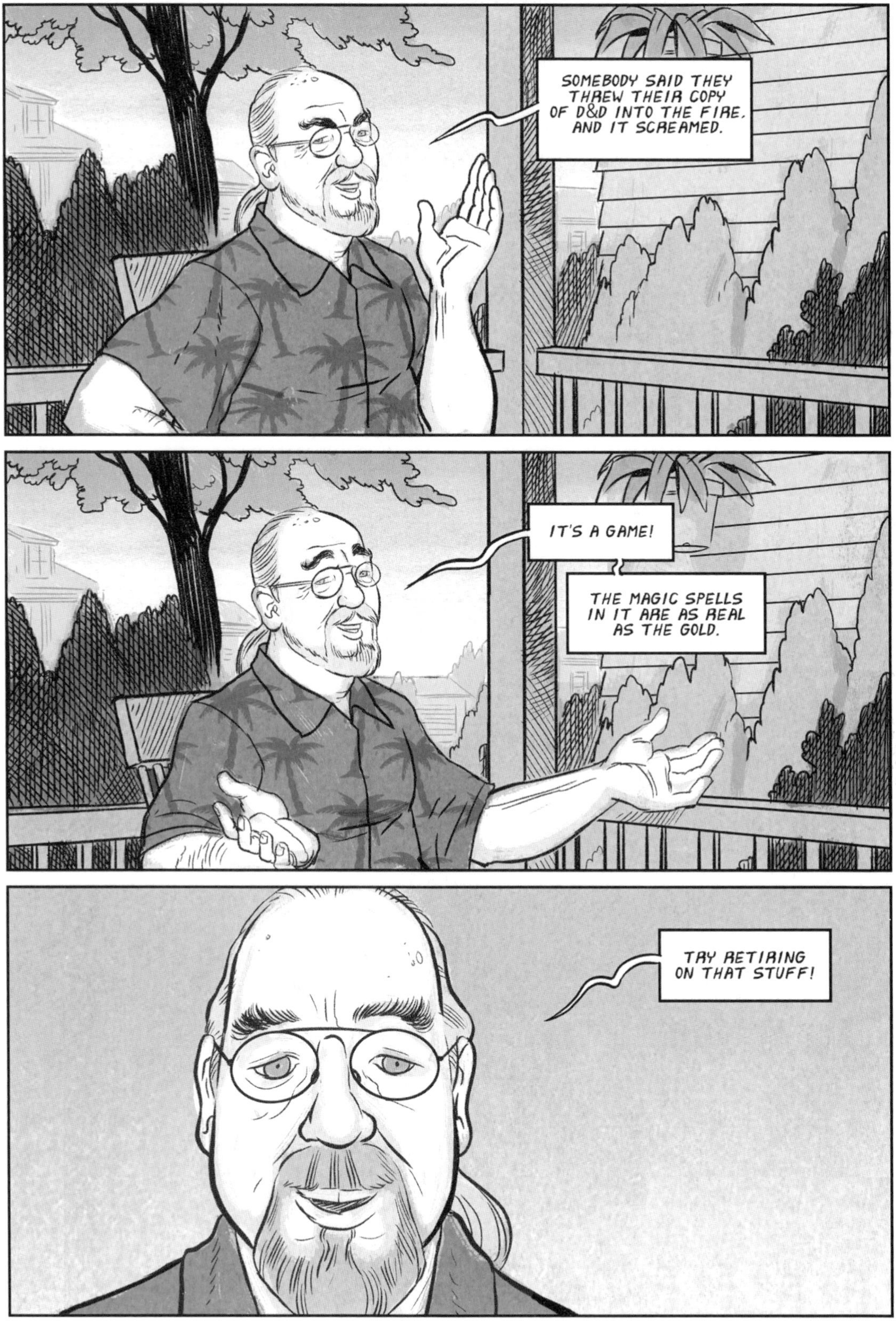

SOMEBODY SAID THEY THREW THEIR COPY OF D&D INTO THE FIRE, AND IT SCREAMED.
IT'S A GAME!
THE MAGIC SPELLS IN IT ARE AS REAL AS THE GOLD.
TRY RETIRING ON THAT STUFF!

CHAPTER SEVEN

YOU ARE GARY GYGAX.

CONAN THE BARBARIAN

AS THE CAMPAIGNS AGAINST D&D GREW, CALLS FROM DIE-HARD GAMERS TO YOUR OFFICE ARE REPLACED WITH DEATH THREATS.

RRRRING!!!

IS THIS GARY GYGAX?

YES, WHO'S CALLING?

IF YOU WANNA GO TO HELL, I CAN SEND YOU THERE FAST, YOU MONSTER!

SLAM!

YOU HIRE PROTECTION.

WHO'S THIS GUY?

MY BODYGUARD.

ARNESON BELIEVES THE HYSTERIA SURROUNDING THE GAME WILL END IMMEDIATELY IF KIDS WILL JUST INVITE THEIR PARENTS TO WATCH AS THEY PLAY.

THEY WILL UNDERSTAND THAT ANYTHING THIS NERDY CAN'T POSSIBLY LEAD TO BEING POSSESSED BY THE DEVIL.

THE PUBLICITY HAS A PREDICTABLE EFFECT: IN 1982, TSR'S ANNUAL D&D SALES SHOOT UP TO $16 MILLION.

16,000,000

THIS GAME OF MATH, MAPS, AND PROBABILITY HAS ACQUIRED AN AURA OF THE DANGEROUS AND FORBIDDEN.

WE COULDN'T PRINT THE STUFF FAST ENOUGH.

YOU PLAY A REAL-LIFE BUSINESS GAME CALLED BRAND EXTENSION.

YOU GO TO CALIFORNIA TO TRY TO EXPAND D&D INTO OTHER MEDIA.

YOU HAVE SOME SUCCESS:

LAUNCHING A SATURDAY MORNING CARTOON BASED ON THE GAME.

YOUR VOICE ACTORS INCLUDE CAST MEMBERS FROM "EIGHT IS ENOUGH" AND "HAPPY DAYS,"

AS WELL AS FRANK WELKER, AKA MEGATRON, FROM "TRANSFORMERS."

THE CARTOON IS POPULAR;

IT REMOVES SOME OF THE STIGMA FROM THE GAME.

BUT YOU NEED MORE MONEY, AND YOU HAVE TO HAND OVER THE LEADERSHIP REINS TO SOMEONE ELSE BACK IN WISCONSIN.

DO YOU CHOOSE TO ENTRUST YOUR COMPANY TO BUSINESSMEN WITH NO KNOWLEDGE OF TABLETOP GAMES?

WHILE YOU'RE IN HOLLYWOOD, THE DAY-TO-DAY OPERATIONS OF TSR ARE OVERSEEN BY YOUR FELLOW BOARD MEMBERS, BROTHERS KEVIN AND BRIAN BLUME.

THEY KNEW THAT I WAS IN THE MIDST OF A DIVORCE, SO THEY FIGURED I WOULD BE HAPPY TO GO OUT TO THE WEST COAST AND GET AWAY FROM MY EX-WIFE.

THE COMPANY IS IN THE RED.

THIS OFFICE COULD USE A SOFA, NO?

THEY WERE $1.5 MILLION IN DEBT WHEN I CAME BACK.

TAXI

THERE WERE 70-SOME-ODD COMPANY CARS, SOMETHING LIKE $1.5 MILLION IN FURNITURE.

YOU LOOK FOR SOMEONE WITH MANAGEMENT EXPERIENCE TO FIX THE PROBLEM.

WE'RE GOING TO NEED SOMEBODY TO GET US OVER THIS PERIOD UNTIL WE CAN GET POSITIVE CASH FLOW AGAIN.

LORRAINE WILLIAMS, THE MOTHER OF A WRITER YOU MET IN HOLLYWOOD, HAS MANAGEMENT EXPERIENCE, AND YOU BRING HER ON BOARD.

BUT WILLIAMS SOON BUYS OUT THE SHARES OF THE BLUMES,

AND SUDDENLY YOU NO LONGER HAVE A CONTROLLING STAKE IN TSR!

YOUR RELATIONSHIP WITH ARNESON STRAINS TO THE BREAKING POINT AS WELL.

YOU HAD BOTH AGREED AT THE OUTSET TO SHARE CREDIT, BUT THE PACT DOESN'T WITHSTAND THE GROWING PRESSURES OF SUCCESS.

YOU DISCUSS THE FUTURE OF THE COMPANY WITH ARNESON OVER LUNCH.

THE ROYALTIES WE'RE PAYING ARE TOO HIGH.

IF WE REDUCE THEM, SALES WILL GO UP.

AND I'LL MAKE SURE THAT WE'RE PAID FOR DERIVATIVE WORKS.

WHO MADE YOU THE MASTER?

RELAX, I'LL MAKE IT WORK.

HE DIDN'T AGREE WITH THAT, SO HE SUED THE COMPANY.

A SETTLEMENT IS REACHED, AND NEITHER YOU NOR ARNESON CAN DISCUSS THE TERMS.

HOWEVER, YOU BOTH WILL BE CREDITED AS "COCREATORS" ON THE PACKAGING OF D&D FROM NOW ON.

Created by
Gary Gygax
&
Dave Arneson

THE CLASH OF THE D&D TITANS BECOMES THE TALK OF GENCONS AND ONLINE FLAME WARS FOR DECADES,

WITH YOU OCCASIONALLY THROWING FUEL ON THE FIRE.

HIS CONTRIBUTIONS WERE IDEAS. NOTHING MORE. DAVE CAN'T DESIGN HIS WAY OUT OF A PAPER BAG.

ARNESON, WHO WENT ON TO TEACH AT FULL SAIL UNIVERSITY, A COLLEGE OF GRAPHIC ARTS AND GAME DESIGN IN WINTER PARK, FLORIDA, TAKES THE HIGH ROAD.

WE EACH BROUGHT SOMETHING, AND WE HAD FUN.

WHEN THE MONEY CAME, PEOPLE'S PERSONALITIES CHANGED.

THAT'S ALL I'M GOING TO SAY.

EVERYTHING WENT FINE WHEN IT WAS JUST A BUNCH OF GUYS WORKING OUT OF BASEMENTS.

I WISH THAT HAD GONE ON LONGER.

YOU SELL YOUR REMAINING STAKE IN TSR IN LATE 1985.

I WAS SO SICK OF THE FUCKING COMPANY AT THAT POINT. I WAS GLAD TO GET RID OF IT.

IT WAS GETTING MORE AND MORE SCREWED UP ALL THE TIME.

AFTER UNLEASHING THE DRAGONS IN A BASEMENT BY A LAKE A DECADE BEFORE, YOU NOW WATCH THEM GO.

CHAPTER EIGHT

YOU ARE A TEENAGER IN THE 1970s.

YOU LOVE D&D.

YOU MAP DUNGEONS.

YOU PLAN ENCOUNTERS, ATTEMPTING TO ANTICIPATE ALL THE DIFFERENT WAYS PEOPLE WILL REACT.

YOU ESPECIALLY DIG BEING A DUNGEON MASTER, GUIDING YOUR FRIENDS THROUGH YOUR CAMPAIGNS.

YOU SEE THAT THE FIELD OF ROLE-PLAYING GAMES IS EXPLODING.

DO YOU WANT TO CONTINUE TO PLAY AS A HOBBY?

OR DO YOU WANT TO BECOME A PROFESSIONAL GAME DESIGNER?

IN THE DECADES TO COME, DUNGEONS & DRAGONS TURNS A GENERATION OF GAME PLAYERS INTO GAME DESIGNERS.

THE RULE SET IS PURE POTENTIALITY, AND THE GREATER THE CREATIVITY OF EACH DUNGEON MASTER, THE MORE THE PLAYERS CAN EXTRACT FROM IT.

MANY YOUNG PEOPLE FOUND THEIR CALLING WHILE PLAYING D&D.

GREG COSTIKYAN GOES ON TO DESIGN ACCLAIMED TABLETOP ROLE-PLAYING GAMES FOR TSR'S COMPETITORS,

INCLUDING A ROLE-PLAYING GAME BUILT AROUND THE "STAR WARS" LICENSE.

HE MAKES THE BIZARRE "TOON," A ROLE-PLAYING GAME WITH THE TWISTED PHYSICS AND WARPED LOGIC OF A BUGS BUNNY-ESQUE CARTOON.

THE ABILITY TO PLAY AN INDIVIDUAL CHARACTER IN AN IMAGINARY WORLD WAS ASTONISHING.

SEVERAL TABLETOP COMPANIES SPRANG UP IN TSR'S WAKE: STEVE JACKSON GAMES, WHITE WOLF GAMES, HERO GAMES.

AT THE SAME TIME, ROLE-PLAYING COMPUTER GAMES BEGAN TAKING HOLD.

BUT AS THE STYLE OF GAMING THAT D&D PIONEERED BECOMES INCREASINGLY POPULAR, THE ORIGINAL GAME LOSES MARKET SHARE.

THE COMPANY BECOMES NOTORIOUS FOR ZEALOUSLY PROTECTING ITS INTELLECTUAL PROPERTY.

TSR IS SOON REFERRED TO BY GEEKS AS "T$R: THEY SUE REGULARLY."

BY 1997, THE COMPANY IS DEEPLY IN DEBT, AND IS PURCHASED BY WIZARDS OF THE COAST, THE COMPANY THAT MADE ITS FORTUNES WITH "MAGIC: THE GATHERING," A FANTASY-THEMED TRADING CARD GAME."

WIZARDS OF THE COAST REGAINS SOME GOODWILL AND POPULARITY WITH THE RELEASE OF THE THIRD EDITION OF D&D RULES IN 2000.

GYGAX IS BROUGHT IN FOR A BRIEF AND SOMEWHAT SYMBOLIC CONSULTATION ON THE NEW RULE SET, AS IS ARNESON.

GYGAX DOESN'T APPROVE OF THE DECISION TO OPEN-SOURCE THE GAME.

THE THIRD EDITION OF THE RULES IS MADE AVAILABLE UNDER THE OPEN GAMING LICENSE, WHICH ALLOWED ANYONE TO MODIFY OR WRITE GAMES BASED ON THE CORE SYSTEM FOR FREE.

IT PRETTY MUCH GIVES THE STORE AWAY.

IT RUINS THE UNIQUENESS OF D&D.

BUT THE BIGGEST THREAT D&D FACES IS NOT OPEN-SOURCING:

IT IS THE RISE OF THE INTERNET AND ONLINE ROLE-PLAYING GAMES.

AS THE NUMBER OF SUBSCRIBERS TO MASSIVELY MULTIPLAYER SWORD AND SORCERY GAMES GROWS, DUNGEONS & DRAGONS ADS BEGIN TO APPEAR IN VIDEO-GAME MAGAZINES.

THE AD CAMPAIGN TAKES A STAB AT ONLINE GAMERS.

IF YOU'RE GOING TO SIT IN YOUR BASEMENT PRETENDING TO BE AN ELF YOU SHOULD AT LEAST HAVE SOME FRIENDS OVER TO HELP

THE 4TH EDITION OF THE D&D RULES MEETS ONLINE GAMES HALFWAY.

WIZARDS OF THE COAST LAUNCHES A SOCIAL NETWORKING SITE CALLED GLEEMAX, WHICH AIMS TO BE FACEBOOK FOR TABLETOP GAMERS.

BUT FOR MANY, PLAYING A GAME ONLINE IS JUST A LOT EASIER AND MORE COMPELLING THAN GATHERING AROUND A TABLE IN SOMEONE'S BASEMENT.

BLIZZARD ENTERTAINMENT, THE COMPANY THAT WOULD GO ON TO MAKE THE MASSIVELY MULTIPLAYER ROLE-PLAYING GAME "WORLD OF WARCRAFT," WAS BUILT BY D&D FANS.

CHRIS "THUNDERGOD" METZEN OF BLIZZARD ENTERTAINMENT CREDITS D&D WITH BEING A CRUCIAL INSPIRATION.

THAT COOPERATIVE EXPERIENCE PORTS OVER REALLY WELL TO DIGITAL MEDIA, ESPECIALLY WITH THE RISE OF THE INTERNET.

PLAYERS AROUND THE WORLD ARE FORMING FRIENDSHIPS AND HAVING ADVENTURES.

PART OF THE MAGIC IS THAT IT HEARKENS BACK TO THOSE DATELESS NIGHTS PLAYING D&D.

FOR MANY, IT FELT LIKE THE BEGINNING OF A NEW ERA—AND THE END OF ANOTHER.

CHAPTER NINE

AFTER BEING DIAGNOSED WITH CANCER, DAVE ARNESON RETURNED TO ST. PAUL, MINNESOTA.

HE SPENT HIS FINAL MONTHS GAMING WITH HIS OLD FRIENDS.

HE DIED ON APRIL 7, 2009, AT AGE 61.

HIS DAUGHTER, MALIA WEINHAGEN, SUMMED UP HER FATHER'S LEGACY TO THE LOCAL NEWSPAPER:

YOU GET SO BUSY AND SO DISTRACTED WITH EVERYDAY LIVING, BUT MY DAD NEVER FORGOT ABOUT PASSION AND HAVING FUN.

GYGAX, WHO'D BEEN BATTLING HEALTH PROBLEMS FOR YEARS, DIED AT HIS HOME ON MARCH 4, 2008.

HE WAS 69.

THE NEXT NIGHT, TV HOST STEPHEN COLBERT, A LIFELONG D&D FAN, PAID TRIBUTE IN THE CLOSING MOMENTS OF HIS SHOW...

GARY YOU WILL BE MISSED.

HOW MUCH WILL YOU BE MISSED?

TWENTY!

MAY YOUR PRISMATIC SPRAY ALWAYS BYPASS YOUR TARGET'S REFLEX-SAVING THROW.

DESPITE THE COMPETITION WITH VIDEO GAMES, DUNGEONS & DRAGONS HAS NOW FOUND A NEW ROLE IN POPULAR CULTURE.

THE KIDS WHO PLAYED THE GAME IN ITS HEYDAY ARE IN POSITIONS OF POWER, AND INTRODUCING THE GAME TO A NEW GENERATION.

IN 2014, HASBRO AND WIZARDS OF THE COAST CELEBRATE D&D'S 40TH ANNIVERSARY WITH THE PUBLICATION OF A NEW PLAYERS' HANDBOOK.

THE 5TH EDITION BECOMES THE NUMBER-ONE BEST-SELLER ON AMAZON.

A DUNGEONS & DRAGONS MOVIE GETS PUT INTO PRODUCTION.

ACTOR VIN DIESEL, NBA ALL-STAR TIM DUNCAN, AND PORN STAR SASHA GREY ARE JUST SOME OF THE CELEBRITIES WHO PROFESS THEIR LOVE OF THE GAME.

THE TV HIT "STRANGER THINGS" TURNS ITS D&D PLAYING KIDS INTO MAINSTREAM HEROES.

OTHER POPULAR SHOWS, SUCH AS "COMMUNITY," MAKE THEIR OWN HOMAGE TO THE GAME.

WHETHER PLAYING THE GAME, OR WATCHING "GAME OF THRONES,"

AFTER YEARS ON THE OUTSIDE, IT'S OKAY TO BE A FANTASY GEEK.

AS "VICE" MAGAZINE DECLARES, "DUNGEONS & DRAGONS IS OFFICIALLY COOL AGAIN."

BUT FOR THOSE WHO HAD LONG CHERISHED THE GAME, IT NEVER WENT OUT OF STYLE.

YOU ARE GARY GYGAX—PLAYING WHAT WOULD BE ONE OF YOUR FINAL GAMES.

YOU SIT DOWN AT A TABLE WITH A FEW OTHER REVELERS ON YOUR FRONT PORCH.

THERE ARE BOOKS AND PLANTS AND GAMES NEARBY.

A FAN SLOWLY STIRS THE THICK, HUMID AIR.

YOU PRODUCE A CARDBOARD TUBE AND REMOVE A LARGE PIECE OF GRAPH PAPER FROM IT.

IT IS A HAND-DRAWN MAP OF YOUR OWN DESIGN.

THERE ARE GREEN SWIRLS REPRESENTING TREES, AND TINY BLACK SQUARES FOR BUILDINGS.

YOU PRODUCE AN ENORMOUS POLYHEDRAL DIE THAT'S AS BLACK AS ONYX.

YOU SPARK UP A BLACK & MILD CIGAR.

AFTER MAKING SURE YOUR WIFE ISN'T LOOKING, YOU CRACK OPEN A SECOND BOTTLE OF GUINNESS.

YOU ARE THE GAME MASTER, TELLING THE PLAYERS OF THEIR NEW ADVENTURE.

YOU LEAVE THE CARAVAN AND COME TO A VILLAGE.

YOU CAN STAY HERE AND SEE WHAT'S AROUND.

WHO WANTS TO GO WHERE?

IT'S DAY THREE OF THE 2007 LAKE GENEVA CONVENTION, AND YOU ARE DELIGHTED TO TO BE GETTING YOUR GAME ON.

THIS IS NEARLY 40 YEARS TO THE DAY SINCE THE FIRST UNOFFICIAL GENCON WAS HELD HERE IN YOUR HOMETOWN.

THE OFFICIAL GENCON IS NOW A BIG CORPORATE FRANCHISE AND HELD SEVERAL TIMES A YEAR IN CONVENTION CENTERS FROM ANAHEIM TO AUSTRALIA, DRAWING CROWDS OF 30,000.

YOU RESURRECTED YOUR HOMETOWN ALTERNATIVE CONVENTION, AND IT HAS ATTRACTED A FEW HUNDRED FANS.

YOU HAVE INVITED SOME OVER TO YOUR HOUSE TO PLAY A GAME SCENARIO YOU'VE RECENTLY DESIGNED.

YOU ARE LEADING PLAYERS THROUGH A CAMPAIGN OF "LEJENDARY ADVENTURE," ONE OF THE MANY TABLE-TOP ROLE-PLAYING GAMES YOU CREATED AFTER D&D.

"LEJENDARY ADVENTURE" IS RULES LIGHT.

LIFE'S TOO SHORT TO SPEND 60 HOURS A WEEK CROUCHING IN FRONT OF A TYPEWRITER WRITING RULES.

THE MORE YOU EXPLAIN, THE MORE YOU HAVE TO KEEP EXPLAINING.

USE IMAGINATION AND INITIATIVE, FOR HEAVEN'S SAKE!

AS THE GAME PROGRESSES, YOU VEER FROM THE SCENARIO INTO A SERIES OF ENTERTAINING DIGRESSIONS.

THE RAVEN

WHEN THE GROUP ENTERS A PUB, YOU RECITE LINES FROM MONTY PYTHON.

NOW, ZIS AFTERNOON, WE HAVE ZE JUGGED HARE. ZE HARE IS VERY HIGH, AND ZE SAUCE IS VERY RICH...

AS THEY LEARN OF NEARBY RIVER CAVES THAT MAY HOUSE TREACHEROUS BEASTS, YOU DESCRIBE A DREAM YOU HAD IN WHICH AN AFRICAN ELEPHANT WAS CHASING YOU AROUND YOUR BACKYARD.

HE WAS TRYING TO GRAB ME WITH HIS TRUNK!

AT ONE POINT, YOU BREAK INTO SINGING A POLKA.

"I DON'T WANT HER, YOU CAN HAVE HER, SHE'S TOO FAT FOR ME!"

ONE OR TWO BRAVE MEMBERS OF YOUR PARTY JOIN IN.

THIS IS WHAT YOU THINK YOUR LEGACY SHOULD BE—PEOPLE PLAYING GAMES TOGETHER IN THE FLESH, WITH A REAL, LIVE DUNGEON MASTER GUIDING THEM.

D&D IS NOT AN ONLINE GAME.

THERE IS NO ROLE-PLAYING IN AN ONLINE GAME THAT CAN MATCH WHAT HAPPENS IN PERSON.

I THINK MY GAMES HAVE DONE A WORLD OF GOOD FOR PEOPLE—SOCIALLY, MENTALLY, EDUCATIONALLY.

I THINK THAT'S WHY I'M STILL ALIVE NOW, BECAUSE IT'S HELPED SO MANY PEOPLE.

I ONLY REGRET THAT I WASN'T MORE OUTSPOKEN IN MY BELIEFS.

WHILE IT MAY SURPRISE—OR EMBOLDEN—THE RELIGIOUS GROUPS WHO LONG RALLIED AGAINST YOU, YOU HAVE FOUND GOD.

THE DISCOVERY BEGAN ONE DAY ABOUT 25 YEARS AGO, FITTINGLY, DURING A GAME.

A FRIEND OF YOURS WAS DOING SOME ROLE-PLAYING WITH YOU AS A KIND OF PERSONALITY TEST.

HE SAYS YOU'RE ON A JOURNEY DOWN AN IMAGINARY ROAD.

YOU COME TO A CLEAR LAKE.

THERE'S A DRINKING VESSEL THERE. WHAT DOES IT LOOK LIKE?

IT'S A BEAUTIFUL SILVER CHALICE, ALL ENGRAVED.

I DIDN'T KNOW YOU WERE RELIGIOUS.

NEITHER DO YOU, BUT YOU WARM TO THE IDEA THAT THE UNIVERSE HAS BEEN MAPPED OUT IN ADVANCE BY SOME CELESTIAL DESIGNER.

THERE'S GOT TO BE A CREATING HAND BEHIND EVERYTHING.

AS THOMAS AQUINAS SAID, "OUT OF NOTHING COMES NOTHING."

OVER THE PAST FEW YEARS, YOU SUFFERED TWO MINOR STROKES, A HEART ATTACK, AND A SERIES OF FALLS.

AND, YOU SAY, IT IS YOUR NEWFOUND BELIEFS THAT SUSTAIN YOU.

YOU PRAY THAT YOU WILL REGAIN THE MOVEMENT THAT YOU LOST IN YOUR ARM AND LEG AFTER YOUR MOST RECENT STROKE.

AND IT IS AN EXPERIENCE INSIDE A GAME THAT PREPARES YOU FOR YOUR ULTIMATE JOURNEY, TOO.

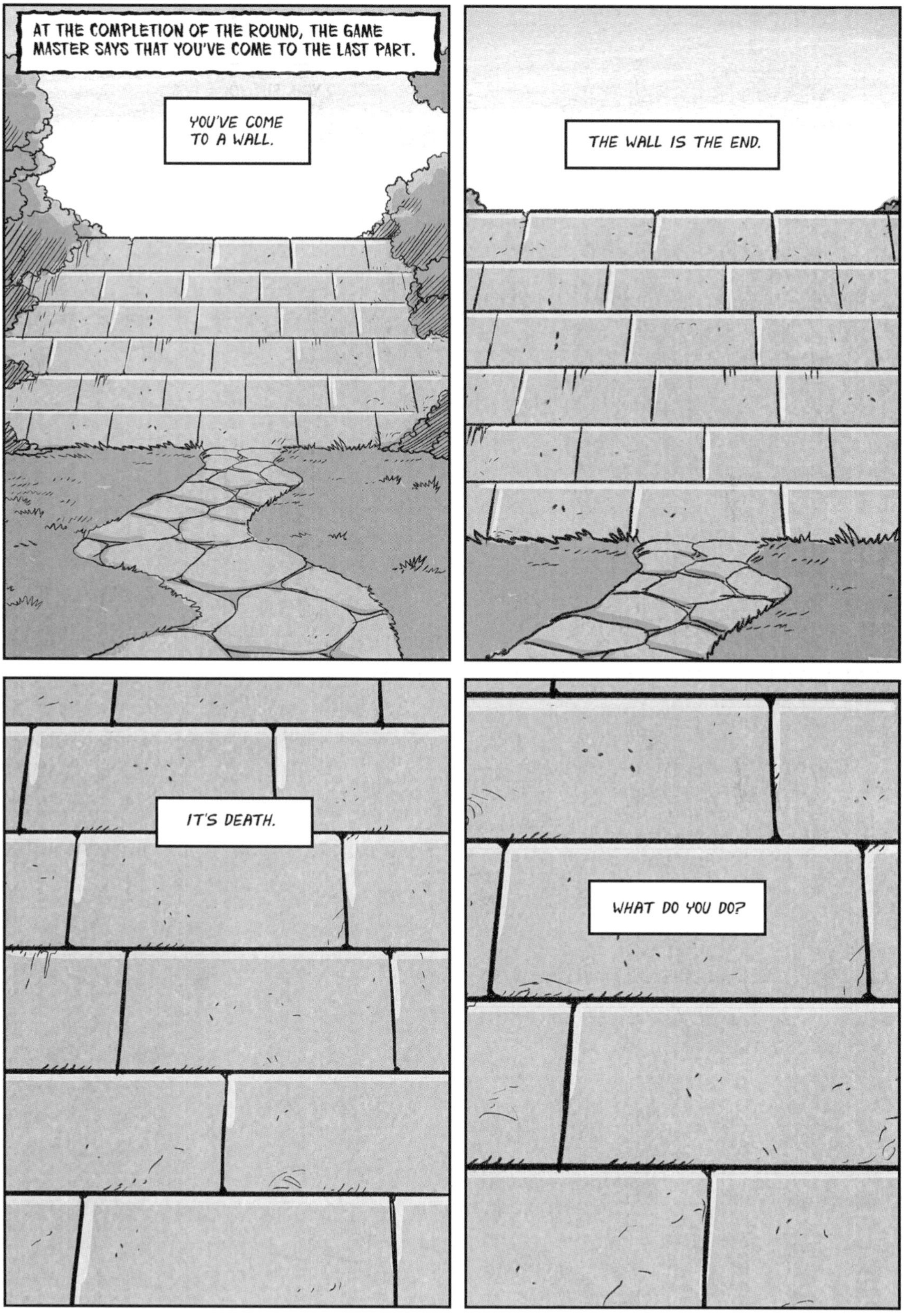
AT THE COMPLETION OF THE ROUND, THE GAME MASTER SAYS THAT YOU'VE COME TO THE LAST PART.
YOU'VE COME TO A WALL.
THE WALL IS THE END.
IT'S DEATH.
WHAT DO YOU DO?

YOU LOOK HIM IN THE EYE.

I JUMP OVER IT.

WHEN YOU COME TO THE END AND YOU CAN'T GO ANY FARTHER, YOU'VE GOT TO GO OVER THE WALL.

GOTTA SEE WHAT'S THERE.

DAVID KUSHNER is an award-winning journalist and author of many books, including three on gaming: *Masters of Doom, Jonny Magic and the Card Shark Kids,* and *Jacked: The Outlaw Story of Grand Theft Auto.* A contributing editor of *Rolling Stone* and 2016 Ferris Professor of Journalism at Princeton University, Kushner has written for, the *New Yorker, New York Times, GQ,* and elsewhere. This book is based on his 2008 *Wired* profile of Gary Gygax and extensive interviews with both Gygax and Dave Arneson before they died.

Illustration by Eddie Mize

KOREN SHADMI is an American Israeli cartoonist and illustrator. His graphic novels have been published internationally, and include *In the Flesh, The Abaddon, Mike's Place,* and *Love Addict: Confessions of a Serial Dater.* His work has appeared in the *New York Times, Wall Street Journal, Mother Jones, Village Voice, Playboy, Washington Post, Wired,* and elsewhere. Koren's work has won several awards at the Society of Illustrators. He teaches illustration at the School of Visual Arts in New York.

Photograph by Liad Shadmi

The Nation Institute

Founded in 2000, **Nation Books** has become a leading voice in American independent publishing. The imprint's mission is to tell stories that inform and empower just as they inspire or entertain readers. We publish award-winning and bestselling journalists, thought leaders, whistle-blowers, and truthtellers, and we are also committed to seeking out a new generation of emerging writers, particularly voices from under-represented communities and writers from diverse backgrounds. As a publisher with a focused list, we work closely with all our authors to ensure that their books have broad and lasting impact. With each of our books we aim to constructively affect and amplify cultural and political discourse and to engender positive social change.

Nation Books is a project of The Nation Institute, a nonprofit media center established to extend the reach of democratic ideals and strengthen the independent press. The Nation Institute is home to a dynamic range of programs: the award-winning Investigative Fund, which supports groundbreaking investigative journalism; the widely read and syndicated website TomDispatch; journalism fellowships that support and cultivate over twenty-five emerging and high-profile reporters each year; and the Victor S. Navasky Internship Program.

For more information on Nation Books and The Nation Institute, please visit:

www.nationbooks.org
www.nationinstitute.org
www.facebook.com/nationbooks.ny
Twitter: @nationbooks